Art Therapy Techniques and Applications

by the same author

Mandala Symbolism and Techniques
Innovative Approaches for Professionals
Susan I. Buchalter
ISBN 978 1 84905 889 6
eISBN 978 0 85700 593 9

Art Therapy and Creative Coping Techniques for Older Adults
Susan I. Buchalter
ISBN 978 1 84905 830 8
eISBN 978 0 85700 309 6

A Practical Art Therapy
Susan I. Buchalter
ISBN 978 1 84310 769 9
eISBN 978 1 84642 004 7

of related interest

Art Therapy Exercises
Inspirational and Practical Ideas to Stimulate the Imagination
Liesl Silverstone
Foreword by Brian Thorne
ISBN 978 1 84310 695 1
eISBN 978 1 84642 693 3

Inner Journeying Through Art-Journaling
Learning to See and Record your Life as a Work of Art
Marianne Hieb
ISBN 978 1 84310 794 1
eISBN 978 1 84642 240 9

Art Therapy and Clinical Neuroscience
Edited by Noah Hass-Cohen and Richard Carr
Foreword by Frances F. Kaplan
ISBN 978 1 84310 868 9
eISBN 978 1 84642 839 5

A Creative Guide to Exploring Your Life
Self-Reflection Using Photography, Art, and Writing
Graham Gordon Ramsay and Holly Barlow Sweet
ISBN 978 1 84310 892 4
eISBN 978 1 84642 866 1

Art Therapy Techniques and Applications

Susan I. Buchalter

Jessica Kingsley *Publishers*
London and Philadelphia

First published in 2009
by Jessica Kingsley Publishers
116 Pentonville Road
London N1 9JB, UK
and
400 Market Street, Suite 400
Philadelphia, PA 19106, USA

www.jkp.com

Library of Congress Cataloging in Publication Data
Buchalter, Susan I. (Susan Irene), 1955-
Art therapy techniques and applications / Susan I. Buchalter.
p. ; cm.
Includes bibliographical references and index.
ISBN 978-1-84905-806-3 (pb : alk. paper) 1. Art therapy. I. Title.
[DNLM: 1. Art Therapy--methods. WM 450.5.A8 B918a 2009]
RC489.A7B764 2009
615.8'5156--dc22

2009003095

British Library Cataloguing in Publication Data
A CIP catalogue record for this book is available from the British Library

ISBN 978 184905 806 3
eISBN 978 1 84642 961 3

Printed and bound in the United States

Dedicated to my creative and wonderful parents,
Bernice and Martin Buchalter

Acknowledgments

To Tracylynn Navarro, MA, ATR-BC, who contributed a variety of creative projects to this book, including Worry Stone Design, Mood Scale Work, Personal Flags, Clay Mandalas, Totem Pole Painting, and Renewal and Recovery Art. She wrote the Open Art Studio chapter. I would like to thank Tracylynn for her hard work and innovative additions to this book.

Special thanks to Dr. Alan H. Katz for his superb technical support.

Contents

Preface

A Practical Art Therapy (Buchalter 2004) was well received and proved extremely helpful for my fellow therapists; therefore, I chose to continue exploring and designing creative art therapy exercises to use with a wide variety of clientele. Art therapy can be presented in many ways; sometimes it is beneficial to have clients draw thoughts and feelings spontaneously and at other times a more structured approach proves to be most therapeutic. There are instances where a clinician may not be sure which approach to take until he or she actually enters the therapy room, observes the clients and assesses their needs. The goal of this book is to provide a variety of therapeutic tasks at one's fingertips because the more tools a therapist has to work with, the stronger and more effective he or she will be. Glancing through this text a few minutes before individual or group therapy provides the clinician with an array of ideas that can be incorporated into the therapy session. The clinician may use the techniques verbatim or modify them to suit his or her clients' needs. I find individuals enjoy experiencing a wide variety of creative exercises; this allows for growth, introspection, insight and problem solving. The clients I work with look forward to participating in groups because they know that each session will add a new dimension to their therapeutic work; they won't become bored or "burnt out" by the same presentation day after day. These techniques are especially helpful when clients and/or the therapist become blocked and need new techniques in order to explore issues in an effective manner.

As stated in *A Practical Art Therapy*, this book is not meant to be a cookbook of ideas. There are suggestions, techniques, applications and goals, which may be used at the therapist's discretion. The objective is to have these techniques incorporated into one's creative schema so that the therapist will be prepared for almost any group and population. I believe it would be very difficult to approach each therapy group, especially if you lead a number of sessions a day, without specific themes and guidelines available. Why not have a collection of therapeutic interventions? Each client and group requires different creative approaches. In verbal therapy some individuals may benefit more, for example, from specific techniques associated with behavioral or cognitive therapy, or motivational interviewing. In the creative arts some clients will benefit more from certain types of art therapy interventions than others. A number of clients might find insight in groups where they draw spontaneously, others might gain insight from collage work or structured open art studio approaches. There is no one special way to lead an art therapy group. The most effective therapist is the one who bases his or her approach on the particular individual's diagnosis, needs and psychological state.

This book is geared toward the practicing art therapist, art therapy intern, graduate student, counselor, social worker, teacher and psychologist. Although certain art therapists think a book of this nature should be geared only for art therapists, I believe that it can prove beneficial for these other specialties as well. This is particularly so since many art therapists are in the process of getting their counselor licenses. The art therapist is specially trained to do art therapy, and he or she is the only individual who should lead art therapy groups, but the other therapists may utilize the ideas presented for their own work, and lead their groups in their own style. Sharing of ideas between the professions tears down barriers and allows for improved communication, enhancement of learning, and better therapy for all patients.

Introduction

The clinician needs to assess which projects are suitable for the people he is working with, individually or in a group. Some of the tasks are more suitable to depressed clients and some may be geared toward seniors, schizophrenic and bipolar individuals. Each therapist must use his discretion when presenting an exercise. A few techniques might need to be broken up into two or three sessions if clients are slow and unfocused, or if there are too many steps involved. Schizophrenic individuals may benefit from more realistic based exercises while depressed clients may benefit from projects that require more focusing and abstract thinking. The therapist may modify the projects to fit the specific need of the clientele.

Art therapy interventions provide a great many goals and benefits. I won't repeat all the objectives in the Discussion/Goals section of the exercises, but the following are almost always present: creative communication, expression of feelings, concerns, hopes, conflicts and issues, socialization, problem solving, and enhancement of thinking and reasoning skills.

I will use the terms clients, group members and patients interchangeably, although some clinicians prefer the term client. In addition, it is politically correct to use he/she, but for simplicity I will be referring to clients as he most of the time.

Topics are organized according to technique or media. Many techniques allow for the utilization of a variety of materials. The therapist must determine which materials are suitable for the population he is working with.

I use a wide range of projects/techniques in working with clients. This keeps the clients as well as myself motivated, energetic, and involved. Experimentation allows for growth and new insights.

CHAPTER 1

Warm-Ups

Warm-ups can be considered "mental stretching." They are usually five to ten minutes in length and help clients become familiar with drawing, and expressing themselves creatively. The warm-ups are relatively simple and provide an almost guaranteed successful outcome, which increases self-esteem and makes it more likely that the client will continue to create. This practice helps convey the message that in art therapy "it does not matter how one draws." It is the expression of thoughts and feelings that is important. The warm-ups may relate to the theme of the main exercise, but recently I have come to believe that this is not a necessity. It depends on the needs of the client and the therapist's view of what the goals and theme of the session will be. Another advantage of the technique is that clients are given time to settle down, relax, catch their breath, socialize and greet each other. Latecomers will not be too much of a disruption because, although significant, the warm-up does not carry the same importance as the main exercise. Warm-ups do not have to be introduced into every therapy session, but they provide an easy and helpful transition into the next stage of the art therapy group. It is a time to experiment with shape, design, and color, and to ask questions relating to artwork, materials, technique and style.

The Finish Line

Materials:
Drawing paper, crayons, markers, pastels.

Procedure:
Instruct clients to draw a finish line (as in a race) and to draw a figure in relation to it.

Discussion/Goals:
Discussion focuses on the placement of the figure (is it placed at the beginning, middle or towards the end of the line; is it at the finish line?). Ask clients to relate

the placement of the figure to their work in therapy, and their physical and emotional health. Goals include self-assessment and examination of objectives.

Moods Warm-Up

Materials:
Magazines, scissors, glue, construction paper, white drawing paper.

Procedure:
Suggest that clients browse through magazines and find one photo that best represents their present mood. Ask them to cut the photo out and suggest they find a piece of construction paper that also symbolizes their mood. Direct them to glue the photo onto the paper.

Discussion/Goals:
Discussion focuses on the reasons each client chose his/her photo and exploration of his/her present mood. How one's mood affects attitude, action and behavior may be examined.

Positive/Negative [I]

Materials:
Drawing paper, pastels, crayons, markers.

Procedure:
Ask clients to draw a positive shape and a negative shape. Then ask them to connect the shapes. Suggest they decide what the newly formed design represents to them.

Discussion/Goals:
Discussion focuses on mood and connection to one's thoughts and feelings.

Stop Sign

Materials:
Drawing paper, pastels, crayons, markers.

Procedure:
Ask clients to draw a stop sign and place something in front of it.

Discussion / Goals:

Discussion focuses on the significance of the object or person in front of the stop sign. Clients explore what is stopping them from achieving goals, overcoming emotional problems, and/or forming relationships.

A man named Ted who was experiencing marital problems drew a large ominous stop sign that says, "Go back!" Near the sign he places his wife and himself; his wife looks unpleasantly surprised and he appears solemn. Ted remarked that he and his wife are constantly arguing and sometimes his anger gets out of control; he curses and says "things I shouldn't." The large sign in comparison to the tiny figures represents "my anger and the problems we are having." Ted stated, "The sign is scary looking; I know if we don't stop fighting we will separate. She won't be able to stand me anymore." He thought that the stop sign was the last warning for the couple to try to get along, and for him to stop screaming and being verbally abusive when annoyed.

The Heart

Materials:

Paper, pastels, crayons, markers.

Procedure:

Ask clients to fold their paper in half. Instruct them to draw half a heart on one side of the paper. Suggest they draw the person they would like to give their heart (their love) to on the other side of the paper.

Discussion/Goals:

Discussion focuses on relationships and the importance of love and caring in one's life.

Draw Conflict

Materials:

Drawing paper, pastels, crayons, markers.

Procedure:

Suggest that clients spontaneously draw conflict using line, shape, color and design.

Discussion/Goals:

Ask clients to examine how the artwork relates to conflict they are experiencing at the moment. Discussion focuses on the size, shape and design of the conflict. Goals include expression of problems and greater awareness of the impact the conflict has on thought, mood, feeling and action.

Draw Your "Zest" (Liveliness or Energy)

Materials:

Drawing paper, pastels, crayons, markers.

Procedure:

Discuss the meaning of zest and then ask group members to draw their zest using color, shapes, line and design.

Discussion/Goals:

Discussion focuses on how one's energy level affects mood and activity. Goals include exploration of methods to increase vigor.

Fatigue

Materials:

Drawing paper, pastels, crayons, markers.

Procedure:

Discuss the meaning of fatigue (weary, tired, etc.) and how it feels to be fatigued. Then ask clients, "What does fatigue look like?" Have them draw their visualization of it.

Discussion/Goals:

Drawing their fatigue provides clients a venue to examine it and not "own it" so much. They can begin to gain control over it by exploring how it affects them emotionally, physically and socially, and exploring what it looks like, how it feels, how long it has been a part of their lives, etc. Goals include development of coping skills and increased self-awareness.

Welcome Mat

Materials:

Drawing paper, pastels, crayons, markers.

Procedure:

Provide clients with a large rectangle, drawn by hand or computer, on a sheet of 8"×10" or 9"×12" paper. Suggest that they create a welcome mat (like the ones usually placed in front of a door) that represents themselves and/or their home. They may write a message in addition to creating a design.

Discussion/Goals:

Discussion focuses on the meaning of the message and design. For instance, is the mat welcoming, does it represent a calm house, a chaotic house, or a depressed household? Clients are encouraged to share thoughts about their home life and how it affects their emotions, attitudes, mental health and satisfaction with life.

An elderly man named Raymond drew an angry looking, foreboding "welcome mat" that clearly expressed his feelings at the time: "Keep out!" His use of dark, bold colors and thick border represented his barrier, the wall he built around himself to keep others out. He was angry because his wife died a few years ago; his children lived far away and he did not have many friends or acquaintances. He disliked television and read very little; he had no hobbies and few interests. Raymond would not join groups or clubs in his community; he would not go to the senior center or go on trips or outings. He shut the world out literally. He was surprised when his peers laughed at his welcome mat; he wasn't expecting that reaction. They thought he was joking. Their smiles encouraged him to smile a bit himself. During the course of the session he slowly acknowledged his negative attitude and unhealthy lifestyle. The artwork served as a vehicle for communication, self-awareness and self-expression.

The Thought

Materials:
Drawing paper, pastels, crayons, markers.

Procedure:
Instruct clients to draw a box and place one thought they want to free themselves of in it.

Discussion/Goals:
Discussion focuses on the thought, its significance, and whether or not the client is indeed ready to leave it behind. Encourage group members to observe the size of the box versus the size of the unpleasant thought. If the box, for instance, is large and thickly outlined, it might mean the client is not ready to rid himself/herself of the thought because it is so well contained. If the box is lightly drawn and the thought isn't too large the individual might be ready to make changes. Goals include working toward positive change and self-awareness.

Clay Shape[1]

Materials:
Clay.

Procedure:
Instruct clients to mold an abstract shape from a piece of "Model Magic" or other clean non-toxic clay. Have them name it.

Discussion/Goals:
Discussion focuses on the design and meaning of the finished product. Goals include expression of mood and feeling, stretching the imagination, and problem solving.

Initials

Materials:

Drawing paper, pastels, crayons, markers.

Procedure:

Instruct clients to decorate the first initial of their first name and then write an adjective that describes them using the initial.

Discussion/Goals:

Discussion focuses on the way the initial is decorated, the colors used, the size of the initial and its significance to the artist. Goals include self-awareness and increased self-esteem.

Smile

Materials:

Drawing paper, pastels, crayons, markers.

Procedure:

Instruct clients to "Draw the first person or thing you saw today that brought a smile to your face."

Discussion/Goals:

Discussion focuses on emphasizing the positive in life and counting one's blessings. Encourage clients to express their feelings as they observe their artwork. Goals include learning to appreciate the beauty and goodness in nature and people, and using this appreciation as a coping mechanism.

Draw Your Motivation to Change

Materials:

Drawing paper, pastels, crayons, markers.

Procedure:

Ask clients to draw a series of arrows representing their motivation to change. Tell them that the arrows might be pointing toward change (the right hand side of the page), away from it (the left hand side), in circles if they are confused, etc.

Discussion/Goals:

Discussion focuses on the way in which the design symbolizes readiness for change, and one's attitude towards change. Explore what type of changes the client would like to make in his life. Goals include problems solving and self-awareness.

The Web

Materials:

Drawing paper, markers, crayons, pastels.

Procedure:

Instruct clients to draw a web (like a spider web) and place someone or something in it.

Discussion/Goals:

Discussion focuses on who or what was placed in the web, how it feels to be stuck, and ways in which the client feels trapped. Goals include identification of problems, self-defeating attitudes, and exploration of coping mechanisms.

Egg Drawing

Materials:

Drawing paper, markers, crayons, pastels.

Procedure:

Ask clients to draw an egg hatching and include what is coming out of it. Tell them to draw something other than a baby chick.

Discussion/Goals:

Discussion focuses on what hatches out of the egg and the meaning it has to the client. This exercise can be considered a metaphor for growth and renewal. Goals include self-awareness and creative thinking.

Some of the items hatched have included: Flowers, babies, puppies and kittens, a dinosaur, a rabbit, snake, and a beautiful bride.

Drawing With Two Hands[2]

Materials:

Drawing paper, markers.

Procedure:

Have clients pick up a different colored marker in each hand and draw something—a flower, face, animal, etc. Instruct them to move both hands at the same time. There are several ways to do this:

1.   Move the markers alongside each other, going the same direction around the form.

2.   Move one marker along one side of the form and the other along the other side.

3.   Move each marker in a completely different direction simultaneously.

Discussion/Goals:

Discuss whether it was easy or difficult to produce this sketch. Explore how it feels to work in such an unusual manner. Relate the exercise to trying new experiences and taking healthy risks.

The Tea Kettle

Materials:

Drawing paper, markers, crayons, pastels.

Procedure:

Encourage clients to describe how they feel when they sit down and have a soothing cup of tea. Next instruct them to draw a tea kettle, but instead of tea pouring out of it have them choose something else.

Discussion/Goals:

Discuss what comes out of the kettle, and its meaning for the client. Goals include exploration of things that soothe, creative expression and abstract thinking.

Some examples of things clients drew pouring out of the kettle included: health, chocolate syrup, gold coins, happiness, love, hearts, and warm chocolate chip cookies. *The idea for this project arose when a client mentioned that she thinks of steam coming out of a tea kettle to relax.*

Question Mark/Problem

Materials:

Drawing paper, markers, crayons, pastels.

Procedure:

Ask clients to draw a large question mark and a symbol representing a problem underneath it.

Discussion/Goals:

Discussion focuses on the size and style of the question mark (is it small, large, black or colorful), and the problems illustrated. Encourage group members to share the significance of the question mark; for instance, if it is large and bold could it mean they are very unsure how to handle the problem; if it is small are they thinking of solutions? Examine the problem represented and its significance. Goals include identification of issues and concerns.

Draw a Halo

Materials:

Drawing paper, markers, pastels, crayons.

Procedure:

Ask clients to draw a halo and place someone under it.

Discussion/Goals:

Ask group members to share who they placed under the halo (e.g. a friend, relative, the client, another group member, etc.). Have them describe their illustration. Discuss the traits that someone would possess in order to be given such an honor. Examine the clients' values and have them list traits of people they admire. Encourage group members to explore and then list their own positive characteristics. Objectives include self-awareness and exploration of values that help connect clients to others.

Movement

Materials:

Drawing paper, markers, pastels, crayons.

Procedure:

Ask clients to draw a series of shapes moving in one direction.

Discussion/Goals:

Discussion focuses on the colors, size and types of shapes drawn, and the direction in which the forms are moving (up, down, right or left). Ask group members if the shapes are moving toward a goal or aimlessly. Have clients relate the movement to their work in therapy and their goals.

Inanimate Object Drawing

Materials:

Drawing paper, markers, pastels, crayons.

Procedure:

Ask group members to draw an inanimate object that represents them in some way; for instance, if the client is an artist, the object represented might be a palette; if he/she loves to bake, the object might be a cake.

Discussion/Goals:

Discussion focuses on what object was chosen and the reason why it was selected. Goals include self-awareness and exploration of leisure skills and hobbies.

Group Mood

Materials:

Drawing paper, markers, pastels, crayons.

Procedure:

Direct clients to draw what they perceive to be the mood of the group (e.g. bright, solemn, silly, tired, depressed, etc.).

Discussion/Goals:

Ask clients the reasons they chose a specific mood. Examine how the atmosphere of the group affects the structure and effectiveness of the session. Discuss how examining the group mood can be used to enhance understanding and exploration of group dynamics. Question clients as to whether or not they have the ability to control and/or change their frame of mind.

Notes

1. Model Magic is a type of clay that is very pliable and pleasant to work with. It does not have an odor and it is a clean clay—color does not rub off on one's hands.

2. Modified from a project presented by Nita Leland at www.nitaleland.com/project/draw2hand.htm

CHAPTER 2

Mindfulness

Mindfulness is very important in therapy because it allows the client to experience being in the moment. It provides peace and calm, and a way to rid the individual of invading thoughts, anxiety and stress, even for a short while. Group members are encouraged to focus their full attention on what they are experiencing and to let their incoming thoughts gently flow away. Accepting one's individual pattern of focusing and thinking is emphasized; group members are encouraged not to judge their thoughts but to allow them to center on the exercise. Clients are supported to acknowledge their uniqueness and use their senses to derive as much as possible out of each creative experience. A significant goal would focus on appreciating one's blessings by staying in the "here and now" as much as possible. This will lessen stress and open the client's eyes to see what he does have; examples include love of family, art, music, and nature's gifts such as beautiful sunsets, colorful autumn leaves, magnificent flowers, full moons, and the scent of freshly cut grass.

Mindfulness Exercise

Materials:
Drawing paper, pastels, crayons, markers.

Procedure:
Ask patients to close their eyes and relax, and listen to the sounds around them (birds chirping, sounds from the heater or air conditioner, wind blowing, etc.). Ask them to just focus on the sounds and let all other thoughts float away. After a few minutes suggest that they draw what they experienced. They may use color and shape, or objects and figures to represent their thoughts and feelings.

Discussion/Goals:

Discussion focuses on the importance of becoming mindful in one's life. The importance of taking time to stop and smell the roses, not dwelling on the past or worrying about the future may be explored. Goals include stress reduction and relaxation.

The Wave

Materials:

Drawing paper, pastels, crayons, markers.

Procedure:

Ask patients to visualize themselves riding a wave at the beach. Suggest they visualize the size of the wave, the speed and color of the wave, the strength of the wave and how they are feeling emotionally and physically. Ask them to visualize the way in which they are riding the wave (for instance, are they on a surfboard, are they actually in the wave, under the wave, etc). Ask them about the water (is it cold, warm, hard, soft, comforting or threatening). Then ask them to draw this visual experience.

Discussion/Goals:

The wave may be used to represent how the client approaches issues, problems and challenges. Discussion focuses on how the client rides the wave; does he/she glide on top of it, dive into it, or fall under the water? Explore how the wave can represent life's challenges, and discuss what specific challenges group members are experiencing. Examine methods to ride "life's waves" e.g. "When hungry can you ride the wave of hunger and wait until dinner to eat, or do you need to eat that cookie right now? When stressed can you take deep breaths, do relaxation exercises and allow the stress to decrease and/or pass?"

Goals include identifying, changing and developing new coping strategies.

The Five Senses

Materials:

Drawing paper, pastels, crayons, markers, variety of objects (listed below), basket or box.

Procedure:

Fill a basket or box with a variety of objects, each of which should clearly represent all of the senses. An example would be a ridged potato chip. It has a distinct smell, you can feel the ridges, it has a salty taste, and it appears oval and somewhat wavy in design. It has a pale yellow color. If you break it in half you can hear a snap. Another example would be a dough ball. It is pale beige, it feels soft and squishy, it also sounds squishy when you squeeze it, it tastes doughy, and it has a distinctive smell. Ask each client to choose one of the objects and examine it for a few minutes. Then direct each individual to explore his or her object one sense at a time. After this is completed suggest that group members draw the object they chose using color and shape. Suggest that they keep in mind the feelings they experienced during the exercise.

Discussion/Goals:

Each group member is given the opportunity to voice his/her thoughts about the exercise. They may be asked to share which sense they focused upon most and the reasons for their choice. Feelings and thoughts about centering on one object may be examined. Goals include learning how to be in the moment, how to let extraneous thoughts pass by, and how to focus on one thing at a time in order to decrease stress and lessen troublesome thoughts.

Body Scan

Materials:

Drawing paper, pastels, crayons, markers.

Procedure:

Lead group members in a full body scan. Have them close their eyes (if they are comfortable doing so) and suggest they relax their eyebrows, eyes, nose, mouth, jaw, neck, shoulders, arms, hands, chest, stomach, thighs, legs, feet and toes. Go through each body part slowly and in a soft, low voice. Soothing music may be playing as you do this. After the exercise ask group members to fold their paper in half. Suggest they draw how their body felt before the exercise, on one side of the paper, and how their body felt after the exercise, on the other side of the paper.

Discussion/Goals:

Discussion may focus on how the artwork reflects the relaxation experience and the changes that occurred during the exercise. Goals include learning how to self-soothe and de-stress in order to attain a peaceful state of being and to help ward off anxiety and panic attacks.

Release

Materials:

Relaxing music, drawing paper, pastels, crayons, markers.

Procedure:

Play soothing background music. Ask clients to relax and pay attention to their breath. Ask them to spend a few minutes breathing in and out slowly. If they feel comfortable have them close their eyes. Suggest that clients visualize what they are breathing out. Ask them to think about size, shape, color and texture. Next ask them to draw "what they breathed out." Examples may include breathing out stress, anger, fear, etc. They may use any type of design to depict their thoughts.

Discussion/Goals:

Discussion focuses on the relaxation experience, the feeling of release when breathing out, and the emotions/feelings depicted in the artwork. Clients have the opportunity to gain a better understanding of their feelings by analyzing and observing the size, color and shape of their design. Goals include release of negative feelings and stress.

Flower Study

Materials:

Paper, pastels, crayons, markers, a flower.

Procedure:

Have clients take turns examining a rose or other flower. Encourage them to study it carefully, focusing on how it feels in their hands. Support them to explore its curves, texture, lines, design, shape, weight and scent. Direct group members to focus on the parts of the flower that are smooth and soft and the parts that are irregular or rough. Then suggest that clients draw the essence of the flower, the beauty of it, using line, shape and color. Suggest that the sketch does not need to be realistic. The picture might capture the mood, feel and splendor of the flower.

Discussion/Goals:

Discussion focuses on the appreciation of beauty and the importance of taking time to explore nature and our environment. Goals include awareness, learning to value being in the moment, and understanding the connection between being in the moment and feeling calm and relaxed.

Movements

Materials:
Drawing paper, pastels, crayons, markers, soothing music.

Procedure:
Place a sheet of 11"×14" drawing paper on a table in front of each group member and have them initial the sheet. Play very soft, soothing music and suggest clients walk slowly around the room, so slowly that each step is very deliberate and thought out. After every few steps have them stop and draw their feeling at that moment on the paper in front of them (somewhat like musical chairs). This may be done once or a number of times. When the clients get back to their original seat ask them to examine the designs/marks and scribbles on the paper in front of them and relate the designs created to their mood and their reaction to the exercise. Ask them to hold up the paper and have group members who contributed to the design share their thoughts about their contribution and/or the overall picture.

Discussion/Goals:
Discussion focuses on exploring patience, connections, and one's place in time and space. Clients may share how they felt about moving so slowly and the images the experience evoked. Goals include increased self-awareness and the power of being in the moment.

Textures

Materials:
Bag full of items (see below), glue, drawing paper.

Procedure:
Present a bag or box full of items that have distinct textures such as sand paper, Brillo soap pads, corduroy material, ridged potato chips or bristles on a small brush. Ask clients to choose a variety of items and take some time experiencing them (touching them, focusing on how they look, feel, smell, etc.). Suggest that clients glue the textured objects on a sheet of paper or cardboard in order to form a design.

Discussion/Goals:
Discussion focuses on the significance of touch in our relationships and in our environment. Clients may share how touch can affect mood and stress levels (for example, petting a cat or dog often relieves anxiety and lowers blood pressure).

Being in the moment allows an individual to enjoy the experience fully and reap many rewards.

Peer Drawing I

Materials:

Drawing paper, pastels, crayons, markers.

Procedure:

Ask group members to team up into pairs and listen very carefully to their partner speak about himself/herself. Suggest that clients focus on their partner's eyes, expressions, voice, tone, sighs, gasps, yawns, body language, etc. Ask them to pay attention to the whole person, all aspects of him/her. Now have the clients draw each other's "core" using color, line, design and shape.

Discussion/Goals:

Discussion focuses on mindful listening and being able to understand and reflect what is really being said. It emphasizes the importance of viewing individuals on many levels in order to develop empathy, and healthier and more satisfying relationships. Goals include socialization and self-awareness.

Loving Breath

Materials:

Drawing paper, pastels, crayons, markers.

Procedure:

Suggest that clients slowly breathe in and out, and imagine their breath is embracing them. Explain that they are being "bathed in peace, love and warmth." Suggest they breathe in beauty and calmness, and breathe out comfort and solace. After this exercise ask clients to draw themselves being embraced by something or someone they love.

Discussion/Goals:

Discussion focuses on how clients felt during the exercise, and the way they designed their drawing. Encourage them to share how it feels to be embraced, and explore who or what embraced them in their picture. Goals include exploration of ways to achieve inner peace and feelings of comfort.

Mindful Painting

Materials:

Acrylics, watercolors or tempera paints, brushes, pencils, paper.

Procedure:

Suggest that clients experience the paint by brushing it on the paper without thought to design or quality of the artwork. Support the clients to focus on the feeling of the brush and paint on the paper. Support them to become one with the brush. Have participants observe the paint strokes, colors and shapes created.

Discussion/Goals:

Discussion focuses on how well the group members were able to observe the experience, feel the movement, and refrain from judgment. Goals include stress reduction, being in the moment, and creative expression.

Mindful Mandala[1]

Materials:

Paper plates, drawing paper, crayons, oil pastels, markers, pencils.

Procedure:

Use the paper plate to create an outline of a circle. Ask clients to fill in the circle from the inside out in any way they desire. Suggest they let their ideas flow onto the paper without thought to a specific idea, figure or theme.

Discussion/Goals:

Discussion focuses on the clients' reactions to the artwork and symbols observed, as well as thoughts that may have occurred while drawing. Have them observe the colors and shapes designed within the circle. Goals include focusing, centering, healing and self-nurturing.

Sand Experience

Materials:

Paper bowls, small items, mostly from nature, such as seeds, shells, pebbles, gravel, leaves, marbles, acorns, little pine cones.

Procedure:

Each client is given a paper bowl filled with sand. Ask clients to experience the sand, feel it, and let it trickle through their fingers. Have them place their hands in it, smooth it out, and use their fingers to glide through it. Then ask them to choose from the materials offered and place some of the items in the sand to form a tactile design. Ask clients to close their eyes and experience their art with their eyes closed.

Discussion/Goals:

Discussion focuses on appreciation of "art for art's sake" (creating just for the pleasure and experience). Goals include tactile awareness, stress reduction, experiencing a different form of art, and focusing on the immediate experience.

Aroma and Art[2]

Materials:

A variety of gentle safe scents such as vanilla, cinnamon, lemon, coffee, etc., drawing paper, markers, oil pastels, crayons.

Procedure:

Ask clients to take turns sniffing the various scents and support them to spend a few minutes concentrating on the experience. After they have tried each scent ask them to draw something that they felt or thought of while they were engaged in the exercise.

Discussion/Goals:

Discussion focuses on the feelings and thoughts that arose while participating in the exercise, and the art that was created as a result of the experience. Goals include greater awareness and self-focus.

Notes

1.   The Sanskrit word mandala means circle. It has held spiritual and ritual significance for centuries, and has been used for healing, unity and centering, and meditation. Mandalas are believed to lead to wholeness in personality, instilling a sense of oneness.

2.   Before engaging in this exercise make sure clients are not allergic and/or do not have an aversion to scents.

CHAPTER 3

Drawing

Drawing allows the client the opportunity to communicate thoughts, feelings, concerns, problems, wishes, hopes, dreams and desires in a relatively non-threatening manner. It serves as a vehicle to express unconscious as well as conscious issues and beliefs. Creative expression provides the individual with the freedom to represent his inner and outer world in any way he chooses. It also gives him the chance to reconcile the two worlds with an artistic dialogue. There are no judgments and the client is told that any way he chooses to draw is perfectly acceptable. The individual is informed he may use stick figures, line, color, shape, abstractions or realism to portray his thoughts. A variety of drawing materials are usually available depending on the population and clientele participating in the session. I usually provide two different sizes of paper (11"×14" and 9"×12"), markers, crayons, pastels and sometimes colored pencils if the group members ask for them, and the participants are not too rigid. In this way clients can make decisions as to the tools they want to create with; this translates into enhanced decision making in other areas of life as well.

Sometimes the groups are spontaneous and clients are instructed to draw anything that comes to mind, or they are asked to draw something related to what occurred in an earlier process group. Many times, however, the groups are more structured and a directive is offered. The directives provide structure, but the participant is free to follow or modify the directive. Clients are usually more willing to begin creating with a more structured approach. Seniors who are reluctant to draw will usually participate if there is some sort of organization to the paper, such as a pre-drawn circle on it. The exception to this is the individual who has an art background; they often prefer to create their own designs.

Taking time during the session to discuss the artwork allows the clients to observe, analyze and relate to representations and figures illustrated. It allows for group interaction and feedback from others. Group members are able to reflect on the symbols drawn, and thoughts may be conveyed that would otherwise not be shared verbally. The drawings benefit the client in a variety of ways: they are concrete so the client is not able to deny representing a certain concept because it is right in front of him; they may be saved and referred back to during the course of therapy; and they serve as a compilation of feelings, problems, concerns and solutions that are exclusively the client's own. Images serve as vehicles, which facilitate communication, growth and insight.

Questioning

Materials:
Markers, crayons, drawing paper.

Procedure:
The therapist draws a large question mark over a square or rectangle (Xeroxed copies are easier) and the paper is given to the clients. Clients are asked to fill in the square with something in their life they are pondering, questioning and/or are in doubt about.

Discussion/Goals:
Discussion focuses on exploring issues associated with the unknown, and examining methods to handle uncertainty about future events. Concerns and issues are further clarified.

People In Your Life

Materials:
Drawing paper, markers, crayons.

Procedure:
Ask clients to draw someone in their life with whom they want to improve their relationship.

Discussion/Goals:
Discussion may focus on problematic relationships, connections, unfinished life business, wants and needs. Healthy and effective methods of relating to others may be examined.

Personal Brochure

Materials:
Drawing paper, markers, crayons, pastels, brightly colored construction paper.

Procedure:

Have clients fold the paper in threes (like a tri-fold brochure). Instruct clients to decorate the front flap with their name and a design that represents them in some way. Then have them open the brochure and on the inside (first third of the flap) have them draw a strength, in the middle inside of the brochure have them draw positive memories and/or experiences, and on the outer third of the inside of the brochure ask them to draw what they have to give to others (feelings, emotions, skills, personal things, etc.). On the back of the brochure suggest clients draw a goal for the future.

This project may be divided into two or three sessions if more time is needed to draw and discuss the artwork.

Discussion/Goals:

Encourage clients to share their brochure with others as a way of connecting, and sharing positive characteristics, strengths and objectives. Goals include increased self-esteem, socialization and identification of feelings.

Empty/Full

Materials:

Drawing paper, markers, crayons, pastels.

Procedure:

Ask clients to fold their paper in half and draw themselves *empty* on one side of the paper and *full* on the other side of the paper. Encourage group members to interpret for themselves what it means to be empty and what it means to be full (e.g. it can be in terms of food, emotions, love, etc.).

Discussion/Goals:

Discussion focuses on how one views his/her life: Is it complete and fulfilling? Does it need improvement or does the client feel empty, hopeless and discontented? Procedures of finding meaning in life may be explored.

Ideal Family

Materials:

Drawing paper, pastels, markers, crayons.

Procedure:

Instruct clients to draw the ideal family. Encourage them to think about where they would live, how many children they would have, how old the family members would be, how they would interact, what they would look like, and what types of jobs they would have, etc.

Discussion/Goals:

Discussion focuses on the family created and the similarities and/or differences between the fictitious family and the client's family. Explore family relationships and communication within the family. Goals include increased awareness about one's role in the family and attitudes and behaviors that affect family dynamics.

Change I

Materials:

Drawing paper, pastels, crayons, markers.

Procedure:

Ask clients to fold their paper in half. Have them draw things they can't change (e.g. their age, perhaps a physical disability) on one side of the paper and things they can change (e.g. attitude, mood) on the other side of the paper.

Discussion/Goals:

Individuals often focus on what they can't change and aren't in control of in their life. This exercise helps clients to observe the differences between what is and what is not changeable. It helps them refocus by becoming aware of self-defeating thoughts and behaviors, and then transforming negative behaviors into more positive ones. Clients begin to understand what to accept and what to challenge in their life.

Life Essentials

Materials:

Drawing paper, pastels, crayons, markers.

Procedure:

Direct clients to draw five things they "can't live without." Emphasize that they can be concepts such as love or happiness, persons, places and/or things.

Discussion/Goals:

Discussion focuses on the items chosen, the order of these items, and their importance. Evaluation of needs and desires, and examination of goals may be focused upon. Goals include self-awareness and self-assessment.

Peer Drawing II

Materials:
Drawing paper, markers, crayons, pastels.

Procedure:
Clients are asked to draw the person sitting next to them using only color, lines and shapes. They are encouraged to be totally abstract (so as not to be too threatening). They are asked to think about the person's attitude and personality when approaching this task.

Discussion/Goals:
Discussion focuses on the similarities and differences between how we see ourselves and how others see us. One's attitude and self-esteem may be explored. Goals include exploration of self and connecting with peers.

Relationships I[2]

Materials:
Pre-drawn figures, markers, crayons, pastels, pencils, pens, drawing paper.

Procedure:
Group members are provided with a large stick figure (approximately 8"×10"). They are asked to complete the figure (add a face, hair, etc.). Then, on the same sheet of paper, clients are instructed to write down the characteristics that they look for in a person with whom they'd like to have a relationship. Lines may be drawn near the figure beforehand to make this easier (even easier if the figure and lines are created using the computer).

Discussion/Goals:
Discussion focuses on questions such as:

1. What personality characteristics are important to you?

2. What physical characteristics are important?

3. What type of person do you usually find appealing?

4. What types of relationships have you had in the past?

5. How were you treated in your past relationship/s and how did you treat the other person?

6. Were the relationships to your satisfaction?

7. Discuss your ideal relationship. How realistic is such a relationship? Explore possible ways to achieve it.

Goals include gaining insight and learning to take responsibility for the success and/or failure of one's relationships. Exploring ways to improve relationships may be emphasized.

Survivor

Materials:

Drawing paper, markers, crayons.

Procedure:

Clients draw a person (preferably themselves) as a survivor. It could be the survivor of an accident, relationship, illness etc. The pictures, with permission from the artists, are dispersed so that everyone is given someone else's picture. Clients are then asked to write five reasons why the survivor in the picture should continue to strive to survive. In addition, the survivor's positive characteristics may be written under the picture, and then given back to the artist for examination and discussion.

Discussion/Goals:

Discussion focuses on independence, stamina and attitude. Group members are encouraged to examine their endurance, strengths and survival skills. Goals include awareness of individual power and courage, and examination of coping techniques.

Mandalas: Emotions

Materials:

Paper plate, paper, markers, crayons, pastels, drawing paper, pencils.

Procedure:

Group members trace the outline of a circle from a paper plate and discuss what a mandala may represent. Mandala is Sanskrit for circle and in the therapy group is used as a symbol for focusing and healing. Clients are asked to fill in the mandala with colors and shapes that represent various emotions they are experiencing or have experienced in the past.

Discussion/Goals:

Goals include healing, focusing, stress reduction, and expression of emotions that may be too difficult to discuss verbally. Boundaries and appropriate expression of feelings may be explored.

A Brief Summary of the Decades of My Life[3]

Materials:

Paper, pastels, crayons, markers, booklet (see below).

Procedure:

Clients are given a stapled booklet (made from 9"×12" paper) that has the decades between 1920 and 2000 printed on top of each individual page. The decades included depend on the average ages of the clients. Group members are directed to draw symbols, people, places and things that are representative of their life during each decade.

Discussion/Goals:

Discussion focuses on important events in one's life. Explorations of experiences, both positive and negative, are examined. Conversation may focus on how to use past strengths and experiences to deal better with present and future challenges.

Goals include reinforcement of one's identity, enhancement of self-esteem, and realistic assessment of accomplishments.

"Who Would I Be Without My Anxiety?"

Materials:

Drawing paper, pastels, crayons, markers.

Procedure:

Instruct clients to fold their paper in thirds. Ask that they draw themselves holding on to their anxiety on the first third of the page, releasing their anxiety on the second third of the page, and on the last third of the page ask them to draw themselves anxiety free.

Discussion/Goals:

Discussion focuses on the role that anxiety plays in one's life. The use of anxiety as an excuse to avoid life's challenges may be examined. One's incentive to release anxiety and methods to let it go may be examined. Goals include learning to live and value oneself as an emotionally secure individual.

Sky Diving

Materials:

Drawing paper, pastels, crayons, markers.

Procedure:

Ask group members to draw themselves about to sky dive out of a plane. It is their first time doing this. The count down is on... 5, 4, 3, 2... now ask participants to draw what happens next.

Discussion / Goals:

Discussion focuses on whether or not the person jumps, how it feels if she jumps (physical and emotional experiences in the air), and how the landing feels (does the parachute get caught in a tree, is it a bumpy or smooth landing?). The drawing and associations to it may be used to explore how clients take on new challenges. Coping skills are emphasized.

Clouds I

Materials:

Drawing paper, pastels, crayons, markers.

Procedure:

Draw a maze of clouds. Include what might be in and/or at the end of the maze. You may or may not include yourself in the picture.

Discussion / Goals:

Discussion focuses on how the clouds are drawn (size, shape, amount of clouds, etc.) and the description of the clouds (are they soft and fluffy or thick and difficult to walk through, etc.). Participants will relate the cloud maze to their life maze. How they draw and relate to the cloud maze may reflect how they are approaching present issues.

Clouds II

Materials:

Drawing paper, pastels, crayons, markers.

Procedure:

Ask participants to visualize themselves in a plane high up in the air. The ride is pleasant and smooth; the sky is light blue. Gradually the clouds become prevalent and there is a thick mist. All of a sudden they feel a jolt; there is much turbulence and the plane starts rocking and making strange noises. Now ask group members to draw what happens next.

Discussion/Goals:

Discussion focuses on how each individual handles the situation. Does he panic; does she hold on for dear life? Does the person jump out of the plane? Does he ignore the turbulence and continue reading his book? Does she hold on to the person next to her or console the person next to her? Group members will be asked to relate how they handle this problem to how they handle challenges and predicaments in their own life. Do they panic, take problems in stride, reach out to others, etc?

The Unknown

Materials:

Drawing paper, pastels, crayons, markers.

Procedure:

Direct group members to fold their paper in half. Ask them to imagine themselves walking through a dark wooded area. Ask them to think about how they are feeling, what they are seeing, touching, hearing and experiencing. Suggest that they draw what is behind them on the first half of the paper and what is in front of them on the second half of the paper. Leave the suggestion vague so that they may include whatever they wish in the picture.

Discussion/Goals:

Discussion focuses on the figures/symbols clients chose to draw. For example, did the individual draw a bear behind him/her, or a pot of gold in front of him/her? Clients may be encouraged to relate what they sketched behind them to their past and what they sketched in front of them to their future. Discussion may include how clients have handled previous situations, are handling their present situation, and thoughts about the future. Coping skills will be explored.

Lost and Found

Materials:

Drawing paper, pastels, crayons, markers.

Procedure:

Ask group members to fold their paper in half. On one side of the paper ask clients to draw something in life they have lost. On the other side of the paper ask them to draw something in life they have found. Examples might include: losing a friend but finding a husband, losing a job but finding a new profession.

Discussion/Goals:

"Life is a process where there will always be change, losses and gains." Clients are supported to examine their gains and losses, and reflect on how they impacted their life. Group members are encouraged to explore the ways in which they react to life's trials and tribulations, and to understand that their reactions are within their control.

Who Am I?[4]

Materials:

Drawing paper, pastels, crayons, markers.

Procedure:

Ask clients to draw an answer to the question, "Who Am I?" Individuals may answer the question in any manner they please (realistically, abstractly, using stick figures, etc.).

Discussion/Goals:

Discussion focuses on exploring one's interests, personality and unique characteristics. Goals include increasing self-awareness and self-esteem.

Present and Future

Materials:

Drawing paper, pastels, crayons, markers.

Procedure:

Suggest that clients draw life as it is on one side of the paper and life if "you felt well" on the other side of the paper.

Discussion/Goals:

Discussion focuses on exploring the obstacles individuals encounter while struggling with depression, anxiety and other mental illness. Goals include increasing self-awareness by examining the differences between one's present circumstances and his/her ideal circumstances. Implementing a plan of action toward recovery may be focused upon.

Feelings

Materials:

Drawing paper, pastels, crayons, markers.

Procedure:

Ask clients to fold their paper into thirds. On the first third suggest they draw someone they have felt positive about in the past and/or are feeling positive about right now, on the second third of the paper ask them to draw someone they have felt neutral toward in the past and/or feel neutral toward right now, and on the last third of the paper ask them to draw someone they feel negative toward right now and/or felt negative about in the past.

Discussion/Goals:

Discussion focuses on how attraction and/or aversion to various personality characteristics affect the clients' relationships with family, friends, peers and associates. Characteristics such as rigidity, perfectionism and negativism may be explored. Goals include self-awareness and tolerance of others.

Memories

Materials:

Eight-inch diameter doilies (or larger), pastels, crayons, markers.

Procedure:

Ask clients to fill the doily in with a beautiful memory. The lovely, intricate design of the doily lends itself to thoughts about births, marriages and other special occasions.

Discussion/Goals:

Discussion focuses on joyful experiences and wonderful thoughts about the past. Clients are encouraged to focus on the positive and explore methods to attain happiness and fulfillment in their lives.

Best and Worst Self

Materials:

Drawing paper, pastels, crayons, markers.

Procedure:

Direct clients to fold their paper in half and draw themselves at their best on one side of the paper and at their worst on the other side of the paper.

Discussion/Goals:

Discussion focuses on exploring one's mood, feelings and attitudes. Examining how the client sees himself/herself at the moment is a most important goal. Questions such as: "Are you presently you at your best, worst or somewhere in the middle?" and "When was the last time you were at your best/worst?" lend for much insight and conversation.

Burdens

Materials:

Drawing paper, pastels, crayons, markers.

Procedure:

Direct group members to draw themselves with their burdens piled on their shoulders. Suggest that the burdens may be physical and/or emotional; examples include financial problems, depression, taking care of a sick relative, etc. Emphasize that the burdens may be depicted realistically or abstractly using line, shape and color.

Discussion/Goals:

Discussion focuses on the amount of burdens and the effect the burdens have on each individual's life. The way in which the burdens and the shoulders are depicted will assist in assessing the strength of the burdens as well as the strength of the individual. Questions to ponder may include:

1.   the amount of burdens represented

2.   the size of the burdens versus the size of the shoulders

3.   the size of the shoulders; strong shoulders, for example, might indicate a greater ability to carry a larger load than narrowly drawn shoulders.

Goals include exploring methods of dealing with one's problems and responsibilities. Frequently clients do not recognize their attributes. When they observe drawings of strong, large shoulders, for example, they often acknowledge that they have not been giving themselves credit for past achievements and strengths. Narrow shoulders, on the other hand, may help clients understand the need to increase their emotional strength and work toward acquiring better coping skills.

Stress I

Materials:

Drawing paper, pastels, crayons, markers.

Procedure:

Direct clients to draw things that stress them. Suggest that they may include people, places and other physical and emotional stressors in their life. It would be beneficial if clients included at least two stressors in their artwork.

Discussion/Goals:

Discussion focuses on the way in which the stressors are depicted, the type of stressors, their size, shape, etc. The artwork allows clients to view and measure their stressors in terms of significance and achievability by observing many of these factors. Goals include examining challenges and exploring coping mechanisms.

Summary of Your Life

Materials:

Drawing paper, pastels, crayons, markers.

Procedure:

Suggest that clients draw a summary of their life on a large sheet of drawing paper. Ask them to include childhood, youth and later years (depending on the client's age). They may fold the paper in thirds, fourths or sixths and depict their life in an orderly manner or create an abstraction. When clients are finished, the person sitting next to them will be given the opportunity to interpret it for the group members. The artist will first give permission for this to be done and then correct the interpreter if needed and answer questions from participants.

Discussion/Goals:

Discussion focuses on the client's representation of his life, his achievements, pitfalls, problems and aspirations. Goals include self-awareness and socialization. Connections take place as group members interact closely with one another and assist in examining each other's life.

Outer/Inner

Materials:

Drawing paper, pastels, crayons, markers, paper plate.

Procedure:

Ask group members to draw a circle. They may trace around a paper plate. Suggest they draw themselves engaging in an activity inside or outside of the circle.

Discussion/Goals:

Discussion focuses on the activity depicted and whether the client chose to draw herself inside (dependence, comfort) or outside (independence, adventurousness) of the circle, and the significance of this. Goals include exploring energy levels and leisure skills, the need for comfort and security, and independence versus dependence.

Upon examining her artwork, an older woman named Penelope stated she represented a friend taking a picture of her. She drew this within the circle. When asked to observe her work more carefully, Penelope noticed that she didn't include herself in the picture, just her friend. She was able to acknowledge that her self-esteem was very low and she was afraid to venture out into the world. She could not see herself artistically or realistically venturing forth into the world. She wanted to stay in the psychiatric program as long as possible.

Swimming

Materials:

Drawing paper, pastels, crayons, markers.

Procedure:

Ask clients to draw themselves swimming.

Discussion/Goals:

Discussion focuses on a series of questions that include:

1. How are you swimming (are you sashaying through the water, sinking, floating, doing the dog paddle, the back stroke, holding on to an inner tube, struggling to keep your head above water, drowning, etc.)?

2. Are you relaxed or out of breath, swallowing water?

3. Are you in warm, wavy, cold, or smooth water?

4. Are you in an ocean, river, lake, pond or swimming pool?

5. Is the water dark and gray or clear green or blue?

6. Are you alone or with someone?

7. Are you content or tense, joyful or sad?

8. Are you drawn tiny, small or large, strong or weak?

Suggest that clients relate the body of water, the way they are swimming and the way they are feeling in the picture to the way they feel about their life and the way they are handling life's challenges.

Draw a Doorway[5]

Materials:
Drawing paper, markers, crayons and pastels.

Procedure:
Ask clients to draw a door.

Discussion/Goals:
Discussion focuses on connections with others, attitudes and self-discovery.
Questions to ponder include:

1. Is the door standing alone or is it connected to walls and/or a house?

2. Where does the door lead? (What is in store for the future?)

3. Is the door opened, partially opened, or closed? What does this say about one's personality and attitude?

4. Is the door large or small; does it seem accessible?

The goals of the project include greater self-awareness and exploration of willingness and readiness to explore options and goals.

Chapters of One's Life

Materials:
Drawing paper, pastels, crayons, markers.

Procedure:
Ask clients to design a booklet consisting of the chapters of their life. Suggest they emphasize *the chapter they are presently experiencing.* They may fold about three or four sheets of 9"×12" or 8"×10" paper in half and staple the pages to create a booklet.

Discussion/Goals:

Discussion focuses on the booklet, but primarily on the chapter chosen. Encourage clients to describe this chapter and discuss their thoughts about it. Suggest they ponder whether they are satisfied with this chapter, would like to go back to a previous chapter or move on to a new chapter. If they want to move on ask them to describe in detail what the new chapter would include and exclude, and how it would make them feel. Goals include exploring experiences and achievements to increase self-esteem and the exploration of needs, desires and goals for greater self-awareness.

Hairdos[6]

Materials:

Paper, pastels, crayons, markers.

Procedure:

Ask clients to draw the various hairdos they wore during different stages of their life (for example, a ponytail as a youngster, pageboy as a teenager, beehive as a young woman).

Discussion/Goals:

Discussion focuses on connecting the hairdos to events that occurred during different stages of life. For example, the flip hairdo might remind a client of the prom, braids might elicit childhood memories. Goals include reminiscing and self-reflection.

Real and Ideal Self

Materials:

Drawing paper, pastels, crayons, markers.

Procedure:

Suggest that clients fold their paper in half and draw their genuine self on one side of the paper and their ideal self on the other side of the paper.

Discussion/Goals:

Discussion focuses on exploring similarities and differences between one's real and ideal self. Acknowledging one's strengths and accepting present vulnerabilities may be explored. Goals include self-awareness and examination of personal goals.

Draw Your Anchor

Materials:

Paper, pastels, crayons, markers.

Procedure:

Suggest that clients draw their anchor (what is keeping them from moving ahead in their life, what is weighing them down).

Discussion/Goals:

Discussion focuses on how long the anchor has been a part of the client's life, the type of anchor, its size, color and weight. Ask group members to share specifically what the anchor is stopping them from accomplishing in their life. Some examples have been getting a divorce, getting over depression and moving to a new home.

A client in her sixties drew a large black anchor on the bottom of the ocean floor surrounded by sharks and other fish. She stated that her anchor has been around for most of her life and keeps her from venturing out in the world and forming relationships. She related the anchor to depression and insecurity, the shark to her mother, and the fish to people who have rejected her throughout the years. This individual had been verbally abused by her mother. The negative statements that were made to her as a child, "stupid, lazy, messy, etc", have stuck with her throughout the years and have kept her from living a fulfilling life.

Control I

Materials:

Drawing paper, pastels, crayons, markers.

Procedure:

Suggest that clients fold their paper in half and draw what's in their control on one side of the paper and what's not in their control on the other side of the paper.

Discussion/Goals:

Discussion focuses on:

1. acceptance of what can't be changed

2. ways to live with one's present situation if it is unchangeable

3. procedures to attain realistic goals

4.   the discrepancy between realistic and non-realistic desires and aspirations

5.   goals include self-awareness and problem solving.

Life's Souvenirs[7]

Materials:
Drawing paper, pastels, crayons, markers.

Procedure:
Suggest that clients draw the souvenirs that they have acquired over the years. Give examples such as postcards, letters, and sculptures from different countries, etc. Hint that souvenirs don't always have to be things; they can be memories, scars, etc.

Discussion/Goals:
Discussion focuses on the importance of the souvenirs and how the souvenirs reflect one's life. Clients usually share more of themselves when they discuss their prized mementoes. Goals include review of past events, reminiscing and self-awareness.

Draw Your Armor

Materials:
Paper, pastels, crayons, markers.

Procedure:
Discuss what armor is and how it has been used over the centuries. Then ask clients to draw their armor (what protects them from outside forces).

Discussion/Goals:
Discussion focuses on how clients use defenses for specific purposes such as keeping people away, distancing themselves from feelings and getting back to their life. The type and amount of armor may be explored (is it large, heavy, bright, cumbersome, etc.). Goals include gaining increased awareness of defenses and exploring methods to break down one's barriers.

In one session a client remarked that her armor was her bible and prayer. She stated she wakes up in the morning and "puts on her armor" in order to be able to get out of bed and dress for the day.

A client named Nancy said her armor was her depression because if she remained depressed she didn't have to face going back to an unpleasant job and an ungrateful and sometimes verbally abusive husband.

A client named Jane represented her armor as her anger. She drew a large figure in bright red and gray (the closest color she could get to silver) armor. She stated that she often is sarcastic, mean and yells at people. This makes people afraid to approach her and then she doesn't have to socialize or deal with her fears, insecurity and low self-esteem. "If I keep them away I don't have to worry about them rejecting me."

Role in Group

Materials:

Drawing paper, pastels, crayons, markers.

Procedure:

Ask group members to draw their role in the group. For example, are they a listener, a leader, the mother figure, the jokester, etc. They may draw themselves within the group setting (for instance seated in a circle) if they please.

Discussion/Goals:

Discussion focuses on the role portrayed in the drawing and how it relates to the client's role in other relationships. Questions such as: "Is it a satisfying role? How long have you been in this role?" and reasons for role placement may be examined. Goals include self-awareness and exploration of relationships.

Counting Blessings

Materials:

Drawing paper, pastels, crayons, markers.

Procedure:

Ask clients how often they focus on the pleasures in life instead of problems and frustrations. Direct clients to think about what is positive in their life and draw their blessings in any manner they please.

Discussion/Goals:

Examine the way in which group members chose to express their blessings and discuss how emphasizing one's blessings can help individuals cope with depression, problems and concerns. Explore how blessings often represent achievements in life such as children, a lovely home, good physical health, etc.

The artwork provides patients with tangible pictures to observe and examine, and refer back to quickly and easily when needed for extra support and comfort. Goals include increased self-esteem and self-awareness.

Reframing

Materials:

Colored pencils, fine tipped markers, pencils, erasers, and 9"×12" paper.

Procedure:

Instruct clients to draw a stressful situation. On a second sheet of paper ask them to sketch one pair of eyeglasses. Suggest that the glasses should be representative of a person whose opinion and views they respect.

Discussion/Goals:

Discussion focuses on the stressful situation, how the client views it, and how he/she believes the person he/she respects would deal with it. Explore similarities and differences in the client's responses. Support group feedback for each stressful situation presented. Goals include increased insight and perspective. Coping skills are examined.

The Date

Materials:

Drawing paper, pastels, crayons, markers.

Procedure:

Begin the session by asking clients, "How do you treat yourselves?" Explore which individuals will engage in luxuries such as buying flowers for oneself for no particular reason, finding time in the day for a bubble bath, reading a good book, and/or cooking oneself a healthy and delicious meal.

Inform clients that they will be creating a piece of art with the theme "Taking Yourself on a Date." Encourage individuals to think about what they would do, where they would go, how they might feel, and the mood they would create on the date.

Discussion/Goals:

Support clients to discuss their date and feelings associated to it. Discuss if their date is reality or fantasy for them. Explore the importance of self-care and self-soothing.

Autobiography

Materials:

Drawing paper, pastels, crayons, markers.

Procedure:

Instruct clients to create the book cover of their autobiography. Ask them to include the title of the book.

Discussion/Goals:

Discussion focuses on the book cover and title, and how both reflect the life of the individual. Group members may be asked about their satisfaction with life and if they have lived up to their potential. Goals include self-awareness, exploring aspirations and self-esteem.

Dancing in the Rain

Materials:

Drawing paper, pastels, crayons, markers.

Procedure:

Read out the following quote: "Life is not about waiting for the storm to pass, it's about dancing in the rain." Discuss the meaning of the quote and ask clients to draw their interpretation of it.

Discussion/Goals:

Discussion focuses on each client's artistic representation of the quote. Use the artwork to explore how clients deal with their problems. Do they dwell on the negative or focus on the positive? Are they able to make "lemonade out of lemons?" Are they enjoying life as much as they could be? Goals include self-assessment and exploration of coping mechanisms.

Transformation I

Materials:

Drawing paper, pastels, crayons, markers.

Procedure:

Instruct clients to draw a negative picture and then transform it into a positive picture. They may add to the image in order to alter it, or create a new illustration next to it.

Discussion/Goals:

Discussion focuses on examining the artistic transformation and then relating it to healthy lifestyle transformations such as changing negative thoughts into positive thoughts and changing undesirable behaviors into more positive ones. Goals include problems solving and taking control of one's attitudes and actions.

The Breakdown

Materials:

Drawing paper, pastels, crayons, markers.

Procedure:

Hand out paper and demonstrate how to fold it into fourths. Instruct clients to listen to the following scenario. "You are driving in your car, merrily going on your way, when it breaks down on a deserted road. You are all alone. The sun is beginning to set and it is getting cold. Now draw what you would decide to do, step by step, in the four boxes provided."

Discussion/Goals:

Discussion focuses on the way in which each client solves the problem. Encourage clients to relate the way they approached this dilemma to the way they approach their own pressing issues. Goals include learning how to work through issues one step at a time, and working towards independence and self-reliance.

The Teardrop

Materials:

Drawing paper, pastels, crayons, markers.

Procedure:

Instruct clients to draw a large teardrop that fills most of the page. Suggest they fill the teardrop with things in their life that bring sorrow and/or have brought unhappiness in the past.

Discussion/Goals:

Clients often have difficulty sharing their grief. This project helps them express troubling issues in a relatively non-threatening manner. Discussion focuses on examining specific issues and problems. Coping mechanisms are explored.

Depending on the clientele and the focus of the session, other ways of presenting this exercise include:

- having clients fill in the teardrop with pictures from magazines (even less threatening)
- drawing one teardrop and one circle or other shape. Clients fill in the teardrop with sorrowful images and the circle with hopeful thoughts.

Push/Pull

Materials:

Drawing paper, pastels, crayons, markers.

Procedure:

Direct clients to draw someone or something they are pushing away from and someone or something they are pulling towards them.

Discussion/Goals:

Discussion focuses on wants, needs, relationships, styles of communication and attitude. Goals include increasing self-awareness and examination of goals.

Draw Your "Scar"

Materials:

Drawing paper, pastels, crayons, markers.

Procedure:

Instruct clients to draw their scar. They may take the term literally or draw problems and/or experiences, that have left their "mark."

Discussion/Goals:

Discuss the differences between visible and emotional scars. Support clients to relate their artwork to their experiences and feelings. Examine the benefits and negatives of having a scar. Questions to ask may include, "How long have you had the scar, how large is it, does it interfere with your life, and how long did it take to heal?" Goals include introspection and sharing "wounds."

The Present

Materials:

Drawing paper, pastels, crayons, markers.

Procedure:

Ask clients to draw the best present they ever received. Clarify that it could be a tangible item but it could also be special words, praise, etc.

Discussion / Goals:

Many clients focus on the negatives in their life. This exercise encourages clients to look at the positive aspects of their life. Goals include increased self-esteem and identifying positive feelings and thoughts.

A client named Gil drew stick figures sitting around a table; he brightened when he reminisced about the time his oldest daughter surprised him with a 60th birthday party. He smiled as he remembered the family and friends that came to celebrate with him.

Another client named Barbara, who drew a bouquet of flowers, shared her delight when her husband came home with flowers and a necklace on their 25th wedding anniversary. She stated she was not expecting anything special.

Customs

Materials:

Drawing paper, pastels, crayons, markers.

Procedure:

Read with clients about various customs and rituals that people have followed throughout history. Encourage group members to share and then illustrate customs they have followed in their own families and communities over the years.

Discussion / Goals:

Sharing rituals is an enjoyable experience, and provides most individuals with a feeling of belonging, and their own sense of history. Goals include increasing self-esteem and a sense of connection to family and friends, and society.

A schizophrenic client named Stan, who is often withdrawn, found pleasure in completing this creative exercise. He shared that as a youngster he ate snacks every day after school and enjoyed this ritual very much. He related this previous custom to his present pattern of relaxing and munching on chips when he gets home from the psychiatric program. Connecting the rituals made him smile and gave him a feeling of connection between his past and present.

Draw Yourself as a Child

Materials:

Drawing paper, pastels, crayons, markers.

Procedure:

Direct clients to draw themselves as a child doing something they enjoyed. Suggest they think about the feelings they experienced at that time.

Discussion/Goals:

Ask clients to observe their artwork, and compare and contrast how they felt as a child to how they feel now. Explore the importance of maintaining balance in one's life and keeping "the child within" alive. Examine methods to have fun and enjoy life such as going to the movies, laughing with friends, appreciating a silly joke, etc. Goals include exploring methods to attain similar pleasurable feelings that one experienced as a child and giving oneself permission to engage in healthy experimentation through humor, games, art, music, etc.

Sophie, a 68-year-old widow suffering from depression, drew herself jumping a rope. She is seen jumping high up in the air with a large, wide smile on her face. She stated that she could still remember the freedom and joy she felt while jumping and the camaraderie she felt with her girlfriends. In contrast, Sophie remarked that she feels "caged in her life now." She stated she is in a rut and enjoys little freedom in her tedious daily routine. She acknowledged that she needs to make friends, join groups and/or volunteer in the community. Sophie looked longingly at her sketch and stated that she has lost the child within and needs to find her again.

A client named Mary drew herself as a tiny figure standing in a park watching other children playing on the swings. She stated that as a child she rarely got a chance to swing because the "bigger" children monopolized the swings. She remarked that life for her is like that now too—she is always left behind.

A 35-year-old woman drew herself feeding chickens on the farm she grew up on and loved as a child. She expressed longing for the fun and freedom she experienced at that period in her life.

Reminiscing[8]

Materials:
Drawing paper, pastels, crayons, markers.

Procedure:
Direct clients to fold their paper in half, and have them draw two of the best periods in their life, one on each side of the paper.

Discussion/Goals:
Examine the periods of time that were illustrated and explore what events had occurred. Encourage clients to share what made them feel content with their life, and explore ways to find some of that satisfaction in the present through realistic activities and pursuits.

Spirituality[9]

Materials:
Drawing paper, pastels, crayons, markers.

Procedure:
Ask clients to draw what spirituality means to them. Suggest that spirituality could include religion, meditation, different ways of thinking, appreciation of family, love, nature, etc.

Discussion/Goals:

Discussion focuses on exploring how religion/spiritual thinking helps one cope with life's problems and provides hope for the future.

Draw a Volcano

Materials:

Drawing paper, pastels, crayons, markers.

Procedure:

Ask clients to draw a volcano in any way they wish.

Discussion/Goals:

During discussion clients are asked if they could relate to their volcano. They may consider:

- Whether or not the volcano has erupted (do they feel like they have erupted?).
- Is the volcano dormant or about to erupt?
- Is it large or small, thick or thin, weak or strong looking?
- When did the volcano form?

- How much lava is in it?

- What would the lava represent?

- Goals include exploration of anger issues and how one expresses anger, for instance, do you bottle it up or let it explode?

Max, a senior who is recovering from anxiety and depression, drew this explosive volcano. It is "vomiting lava" as per Max and out of control. Max remarked that it is a long-standing volcano that has been around for many years. It has kept its lava ("anger") in for a long time but in recent years it has not been able to contain it. Max went on to say that he is frustrated with his finances and with his marriage. He said his wife "is always nagging me, criticizing me, and she keeps tabs on whatever I do; I am sick of it." He remarked that he loses his temper easily and screams and yells at her. She especially dislikes his cursing, which he says he can't control. Max began to explore ways to calm the volcano. Artistically he took a blue pastel and drew over some of the lava to bring "some peace." He acknowledged that he distresses his wife by acting in this manner and decided he might give her permission to "fine him" when he yells. It was decided that a dollar would go into a cookie jar every time he exploded. The money would be used to create an awareness of his actions and to dine in the restaurant of his wife's choosing if enough dollars were placed in it. Max agreed that his marriage might improve if he were in better control and could calmly relate his feelings to his wife.

Support

Materials:
Drawing pastels, crayons, markers.

Procedure:
Instruct clients to draw something or someone (an object, shape or person) that is supporting something or someone else.

Discussion/Goals:
Discussion focuses on who or what is being supported and who or what is doing the supporting. Explore the supports that group members have in their life and the support they provide to others. Examine the ease or difficulty clients find in asking for help. Encourage group members to share periods in their life when they were the supporters and periods in their life when they were in need of support. Goals include self-awareness and exploring methods to be independent.

A client named Edna draw a large boulder as the support and a tiny stick figure (herself) in need of support. She remarked that she is very sad and vulnerable at the moment. She complained that she couldn't make decisions or go anywhere herself. Edna sadly smiled while observing her artwork. She remarked that in the past she was the supporter. She cooked, cleaned, did laundry and made all the plans for her large family. She drove all over the state and felt positive about herself. She stated that she hated this new role and felt guilty about requiring so much from others. Group members helped her acknowledge that there are certain times in life when we are givers and other times when we need to accept help. Edna accepted the feedback but stated she much preferred to be the one in charge of her life and her family.

Three Wishes

Materials:

Drawing paper, pastels, crayons, markers.

Procedure:

Suggest that clients fold their paper in thirds and draw a wish for himself/herself, a wish for a family member, and a wish for a group member.

Discussion/Goals:

As clients share their wishes they become better in touch with their wants and needs, and better able to understand the wants and needs of others. They gain a sense of control and power by "bestowing" such gifts onto others. Often clients project their own needs by selecting specific wishes for their peers; this projection of their needs and desires may be examined. Goals include making connections with others, self-awareness and increase of self-esteem. Procedures of transforming some of their wishes into reality may be examined.

Balance

Materials:

Drawing paper, pastels, crayons, markers.

Procedure:

Direct clients to create a balanced design using various shapes.

Discussion/Goals:

Support clients to relate their artwork to how they balance different aspects of their lives. Examine if the designs are centered, scattered, etc. Questions to ask include: "Do you find you are able to balance your family life, work, responsibilities, and social obligations? Are you off balance at the moment? How can you regain and/or maintain your balance?" Goals include identifying methods to gain control of one's life.

The Fall

Materials:

Drawing paper, pastels, crayons, markers.

Procedure:

Have clients imagine they are walking down a tree-lined street and fall because of a bump in the cement. No one is in sight. It is difficult to get up so they need to be resourceful. Direct clients to draw the way in which they attempt to get up.

Discussion/Goals:

Discussion focuses on how clients choose to help themselves (or if they choose to help themselves). Relate their artwork and associated references to the way they handle their issues and frustrations. Goals include exploration of independence, coping skills and problem solving.

One client decided it was too much effort to get up so he drew himself lying in the street with a frown on his face. He admitted this depiction is similar to the way he handles his real problems; he has no energy to try to solve his problems so he dwells in his misery.

Distortion

Materials:

Drawing paper, pastels, crayons, markers.

Procedure:

Instruct clients to take a familiar object or person and twist or distort it.

Discussion/Goals:

Discuss the artwork and explore what twisting does to an object or person (note that it changes how it appears but it is still the same object or person). Explore the ways in which the clients may feel twisted or confused, and examine how they can untwist themselves in order to think more clearly and become more recognizable emotionally and physically to themselves and others. Goals include self-awareness and problem solving.

Draw a Pet

Materials:

Drawing paper, markers, crayons, pastels.

Procedure:

Ask clients to describe a pet they have now or had in the past. Instruct them to draw either how the pet looks/looked, something about the pet, for example draw a ball if the pet likes/liked to play catch, and/or draw the feeling (using line, shape and color) that they experience/experienced when they were with it.

Discussion/Goals:

Discussion focuses on the relationship the client has had with the pet and the meaning it has/had in his/her life. Procedures to attain a similar feeling by finding something or someone else to focus on will be explored. Goals include reminiscing and getting in touch with positive feelings.

Draw Yourself as a Superhero

Materials:

Paper, markers, crayons, pastels.

Procedure:

Suggest that clients discuss various superheroes such as Superman, Spiderman and Ironman. Ask clients to draw themselves as a superhero focusing on strengths, powers and costume.

Discussion/Goals:

Discussion focuses on the hero chosen, how he/she was illustrated and the reasons why he/she was selected. Explore how the hero's powers serve to help others and then ask group members how they help others. Explore if some of the superhero's strengths are similar to the client's strengths (caring, helpfulness, keenness, thoughtfulness, etc.). Goals include increased self-esteem and self-awareness.

Draw a Grudge

Materials:

Drawing paper, markers, crayons, pastels.

Procedure:

Encourage clients to share the meaning of a grudge (complaint, feeling of resentment, etc.). Suggest that clients draw a grudge they are carrying now, a grudge they had in the past, or that they draw what a grudge might look like as an illustration (using line, shape and color).

Discussion/Goals:

Relationship issues often pose great problems for clients. It is common for individuals to hold onto their anger and not forgive friends and/or family members for past actions. Often black and white thinking (all good or all bad) is to blame for this resentment. It is helpful if clients look at their grudges from "all angles" and better understand how they relate with others. Discussion focuses on the specific grudge, the strength of it, and how long the client has been holding on to it. Questions include: "Is it worth holding on to?" and "How does it help you or hurt you?" Goals include exploration of communication skills, expression of anger and resentment, and self-awareness in relationships.

Draw Yourself as a Stone

Materials:

Drawing paper, markers, crayons, pastels.

Procedure:

Ask clients to draw a self-representative stone. Tell them to think about transferring some of their traits onto that of the stone.

Discussion/Goals:

Discuss the characteristics of a stone (hard, cold, uneven, perhaps unmoving, etc.). Explore how clients illustrated their stone: "Is it large or small, steadfast or about to move, animated or rigid, black, brown or colorful; did they give it a face or is it lifeless?" Have clients relate their stone to the way they are feeling, their personality characteristics (e.g. are they stubborn, unyielding, icy, etc.), and thoughts about their ability to be flexible and move on with their life. Observing and examining the stone often encourages clients to share their attitudes toward change.

Draw Your Challenges

Materials:

Drawing paper, markers, crayons, pastels.

Procedure:

Instruct clients to illustrate emotional and/or physical challenges they are presently encountering and/or have encountered in the past.

Discussion/Goals:

Discussion focuses on the specific challenges and the way in which they are illustrated. Encourage the client to use his/her artwork to understand further his/her attitude towards the challenges and his/her way of dealing with them. Explore whether or not the challenges appear overwhelming, moderate, easy to overcome, etc. Objectives include problem solving, acceptance, goal and action planning.

The Treadmill

Materials:

Drawing paper, markers, crayons, pastels.

Procedure:

Direct clients to draw themselves walking on a treadmill.

Discussion/Goals:

Examine the illustrations, focusing on the relationship between the figures drawn, the size of the treadmill, and the speed the figures are walking. Discuss what it's like to walk on a treadmill (is it difficult, fun, relaxing, stressful?). Explore what happens when you walk on a treadmill: "Do you accomplish anything? Do you reach a destination?" Ask clients to relate how they see their present life circumstances to treadmill walking. "Do you feel you are standing still or working towards a goal?" Examine the ease or difficulty of getting off a treadmill and explore what happens if they do get off the treadmill. Goals include self-awareness, designing a plan of action, and problem solving.

Mountains and Molehills

Materials:

Drawing paper, markers, crayons, pastels.

Procedure:

Instruct clients to draw themselves making a mountain out of a molehill. Tell them actually to include a mountain and a molehill somewhere in the illustration. Explore briefly what this phrase means and how distorted thinking can lead to anxiety and stress.

Discussion/Goals:

Discussion focuses on examining how the size difference between the mountain and the molehill relates to the way clients sometimes react to specific situations where they exaggerate the problem, feeling or situation. Goals include becoming aware of erroneous thinking styles and replacing them with healthier ways of thinking and behaving.

Draw Your Depression

Materials:

Drawing paper, markers, crayons, pastels.

Procedure:

Instruct clients to draw what their depression looks like. Suggest they may depict it any way they please. Have them think about size, color, shape and the impact it has on them.

Discussion/Goals:

Discussion focuses on the power of the depression and the feeling the client has while he examines his sketch. Explore how long the depression has been a part of the client's life, and discuss methods to control it. By observing and examining the despair, the client gains some control back because now he may view it, analyze it and make decisions based on what he observes. He doesn't have to "keep it inside." Goals include problem solving and self-awareness.

Best and Worst Day

Materials:

Drawing paper, pastels, crayons, markers.

Procedure:

Ask clients to fold their paper in half and draw one of the best days they ever had on one side of the paper and one of the worst days they ever had on the other side.

Discussion/Goals:

Discussion focuses on the depiction of the experiences and exploration of the thoughts, feelings and behaviors that occurred. Goals include awareness that life is characterized by change; it has its high points and low points. Group members are encouraged to examine how to balance and accept the good and the bad that they encounter.

Time

Materials:

Drawing paper, pastels, crayons, markers.

Procedure:

Read the following summary, briefly discuss it, and then direct clients to draw time as a shape or series of shapes and objects, or have them represent their thoughts about the passage of time.

"Time goes by much too quickly. I can't believe that it's autumn already. Where did the summer go? I blink my eyes and a week goes by, a month goes by, year after year goes by. It is so remarkable that as we grow older time seems to zoom for most people. Why do you think this is so? Is it because there are fewer new experiences for many of us and less to learn? Perhaps it is because as we grow older we are more aware of time and how precious it is. All I know is that it is essential to make the most of each day."

Discussion/Goals:

Discussion focuses on how group members represent time and how individuals view the importance of time in their lives. Questions such as, "Is time passing quickly or slowly?" may be asked to clarify clients' satisfaction or dissatisfaction with their life. Individuals may be asked how they spend their time and if they are spending it in a fulfilling and satisfying manner. For seniors this exercise may also be used to examine past and present experiences and thoughts about aging.

Draw Your Triggers (for the addicted client)

Materials:

Drawing paper, pastels, crayons, markers.

Procedure:

Ask clients to draw their triggers (what people, feelings and/or things elicit the desire to drink and/or take drugs).

Discussion/Goals:

Examine feelings, thoughts and situations that promote drinking/drug abuse. Goals include identifying triggers and behaviors that lead to addictive behavior, and exploring ways to identify and control them.

Moving[10]

Materials:

Drawing paper, pastels, crayons, markers.

Procedure:

Ask clients what they would have to bring with them if they moved.

Discussion/Goals:

Discussion focuses on cherished items, and the role that personal belongings play in one's life. Explore necessities and luxuries. Discuss recent and/or approaching moves and feelings associated with the move. Goals include planning, decision making and maintaining control over one's life.

Who Listens to You?

Materials:

Drawing paper, pastels, crayons, markers.

Procedure:

Ask clients to draw people in their life who listen to them and support them.

Discussion/Goals:

Discussion focuses on the individuals sketched and their significance to the client. Explore the importance of communicating with others and having your "voice heard." Goals include exploring support systems and recognizing the value of caring relationships.

Feeling Sandwich

Materials:

Drawing paper, pastels, crayons, markers.

Procedure:

Instruct clients to draw a sandwich where the top piece of bread represents a feeling they are open to share with others (e.g. happiness). The middle of the sandwich, the meat of the sandwich, is a feeling that is very strong but usually hidden (e.g. extreme loneliness). The bottom of the sandwich is a feeling that they hold on to, but may or may not be healthy (e.g. feeling no one likes them).

Discussion/Goals:

Discussion focuses on the layers of the sandwich and what they reveal about the client. After clients share the ingredients of their sandwich ask them if they want to leave it alone and not eat it (rid themselves of the feelings), eat part of it (retain some of the feelings) or eat the sandwich up (keep all the feelings). Goals include becoming aware of thoughts, feelings and attitudes.

Wear Out or Rust[11]

Materials:

Paper, pastels, crayons, markers.

Procedure:

Explore the quote "I'd rather wear out than rust out." Ask clients to examine the meaning of this statement and then draw feelings associated with it.

Discussion/Goals:

Examine the artwork and its meaning for the artist. Discuss the differences between rusting out and wearing out. Have clients express ways in which they allow themselves to rust, and methods to change behaviors and attitudes associated with it.

Loss

Materials:

Drawing paper, pastels, crayons, markers.

Procedure:

Ask clients to crumple a piece of drawing paper and then straighten it. Tell them to draw something in their life that has been crumpled (lost or disappointingly changed) on that sheet of paper.

Discussion/Goals:

Discussion focuses on the feelings, behaviors and attitudes associated with the problem. Goals include exploring coping mechanisms and methods to adjust to the loss.

Time of Day

Materials:

Drawing paper, pastels, crayons, markers.

Procedure:

Have clients fold their paper in half and ask them to draw feelings usually experienced in the morning on one side of the page, and feelings usually experienced in the evening on the other side of the page.

Discussion/Goals:

It is common for clients who suffer from depression to say they feel worse in the morning than in the evening. Clients who complain of anxiety will often say they feel worse in the evening, when it is dark, especially if they are alone. Encourage group members to use their artwork to get in touch with their feelings and explore what triggers them. Examine ways to decrease negative and unpleasant thoughts.

Pain Management

Materials:

Drawing paper, markers, crayons, pastels, scissors, glue.

Procedure:

Provide pre-drawn body outlines that fill an 8"×10" sheet of paper for each client. Instruct group members to cut out the outlines and glue them on a piece of paper. Ask participants to fill in the outlines with facial features, hair, clothes, etc. and then place an X next to the body parts where they feel pain. Then direct clients to draw enjoyable and calming activities surrounding the figure.

Discussion/Goals:

Explain to clients that participating in hobbies and other activities is a useful method to minimize discomfort. When an individual is engaged in enjoyable activities he is less likely to focus on his pain, and it usually doesn't seem so intense. Encourage clients to share the activities illustrated and emphasize the attributes of meditation, yoga, drawing, music, journaling, etc. Goals include exploration of ways to alleviate stress and discomfort.

Worry

Materials:

Drawing paper, markers, crayons, pastels.

Procedure:

Ask clients to draw the things they worry about. Next have them circle the things they believe they have no control over.

Discussion/Goals:

Discussion focuses on sharing the things that the client has no control over and the things he does have control over. Examine the fruitlessness of focusing on beliefs and events that one cannot control such as the weather, hurricanes, certain illnesses, etc. Explore the artwork that depicts what the client has control over (perhaps his weight, nutrition, attitude, etc.) and examine ways of focusing and maintaining that control. Discuss the benefits of worry (e.g. attention, superstition: feeling an event won't occur if you worry about it, etc.). Goals include self-awareness and stress reduction.

Step by Step

Materials:

Drawing paper, crayons.

Procedure:

Ask clients to draw a very large shape and then a series of similar smaller shapes next to it—for example, a large circle, the size of a paper plate, and a grouping of smaller circles next to it. Have them color in all the shapes using crayons. Crayons are used because more effort is usually exerted when drawing with them.

Discussion/Goals:

Ask clients how they felt about filling in the shapes with color, and determine the ease or difficulty of filling them in. Discussion focuses on the observation that the large shape takes more time and effort to fill in (often one's hand hurts by the time it is completed). On the other hand, the smaller shapes are filled in quickly and easily, without discomfort. Encourage clients to observe how the larger shape can be broken into smaller shapes, and relate this concept to the importance of breaking down larger tasks into smaller ones. Compare the hand that hurts because the shape was so large to fill in at one sitting to an overwhelming task. Give clients the example, "If opening a pile of mail is difficult to do, just open a few letters a day. Eventually all of the mail will be opened and your stress level will be decreased." Goals include learning how to do things step by step, functioning more effectively, self-awareness and lessening anxiety.

The Tracks

Materials:

Drawing paper, pastels, markers, crayons.

Procedure:

Briefly discuss the phrase "Being on the wrong side of the tracks." Ask clients to draw train tracks and focus on the side they are on. Have them think about whether they are on the right or wrong side and illustrate their choice.

Discussion / Goals:

Discussion focuses on the side of the tracks drawn and what is on that side—for example, are there smiling people, trees, houses and grass there (right side) or people taking drugs (wrong side)? Goals include exploration of where the client is at the moment and goals for the future.

Positive/Negative II

Materials:

Drawing paper, markers, pastels, crayons, cardboard, scissors, pencils, paint, brushes.

Procedure:

Provide an oval template of a face or have clients outline their own. Direct group members to divide the face in half. Ask them to use colors, shapes and design to represent their positive thoughts on one side of the face and their negative thoughts on the other side of the face. Suggest that magazine pictures and words may be included if desired.

Discussion / Goals:

Discussion focuses on the imagery drawn. Explore which side of the face appears dominant, the client's reaction to his/her representation, and the moods reflected in the artwork. Goals include exploration of mood, feeling and attitude.

A clinically depressed client named Jim used paint to illustrate his severe depression and hopelessness. He painted most of the face black and a small fraction of it white. When asked about his work Jim replied that the black represented his darkness and despair. The white represented a tiny bit of hope. No features were included in the image. After further questioning Jim stated that he was actually pleased with his artwork because for at least five years he has not had any hope. He remarked that the last time he had hope was after he left the same program five years ago. It was suggested that Jim try this directive again every few weeks to look for similarities and/or differences in the way he creates the face.

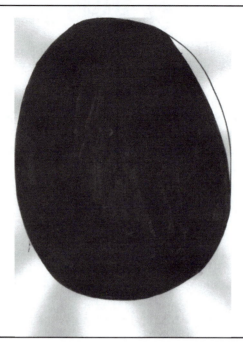

The Wristband

Materials:

Drawing paper, markers, crayons, pastels.

Procedure:

Ask clients to draw a wristband (like the ones worn when a client is admitted to hospital). The therapist may have optional outlines available in case certain group members have difficulty sketching it. Ask group members to fill in the band with symbols representing their thoughts and feelings about being in therapy.

Discussion/Goals:

Discussion focuses on the clients' feelings about their therapeutic work, and/or about participating in a psychiatric program. Explore questions such as, "What does wearing a wristband signify? How does it feel when it is put on your wrist by the nurse? How long do you think it will stay on? Does it change how you feel about yourself when you wear it?" Goals include exploration of attitude toward program participation, and examination of self-esteem.

Life Graph

Materials:

Drawing paper, markers, crayons, pastels.

Procedure:

Demonstrate how graphs may be used to compare and quantify all types of data. Show clients a variety of graphs they may use as a basis for their own. Ask clients to design their own unique life graph representing their experiences, high and low periods, and different stages of their life. Suggest they may add pictures, symbols, words and dates on the graph.

Discussion / Goals:

Encourage exploration of accomplishments, problems and setbacks, negative and positive experiences, and thoughts about one's life. Examine peaks and valleys. Goals include self-awareness and introspection.

Disappointment

Materials:

Drawing paper, markers, crayons, pastels.

Procedure:

Direct clients to use shapes, color, line and design to represent disappointment, how it looks and how it feels.

Discussion / Goals:

Explore how it feels to be disappointed and examine how the clients handle this emotion. "Do they curl up in a ball and retreat; do they become immobile, or do they accept it and work towards a new goal?" Goals include learning how to handle life's challenges and disillusionments.

One individual drew disappointment as a dark shape with jagged, sharp edges.

Peer Pressure

Materials:

Drawing paper, markers, crayons, pastels.

Procedure:

Direct group members to draw a scene representing themselves feeling pressure to act or think in a specific manner. Suggest that stick figures, shapes, and abstractions may be utilized.

Discussion/Goals:

Discussion focuses on the scene illustrated and the way the client portrayed himself/herself. Examine how clients view the opinions of others. Goals include exploration of independence and self-esteem.

Yesterday, Today, Tomorrow

Materials:

Drawing paper, markers, crayons, pastels.

Procedure:

Read and discuss the following quote:

> Yesterday is history,
> Tomorrow is a mystery.
> Today is a gift,
> That's why they call it the present.

Instruct clients to fold their paper in thirds and draw:

Yesterday (their past), Today (their gift), Tomorrow (the future—mystery).

Discussion/Goals:

Discussion focuses on the past, present and future. Suggest that clients review their "present" art and explore ways of staying in the here and now. Goals include self-awareness, introduction to mindfulness and exploration of accomplishments and goals.

Cornucopia of Feelings[12]

Materials:

Drawing paper, markers, crayons, pastels.

Procedure:

Discuss the meaning of a cornucopia (an abundance, horn shaped receptacle). Instruct clients to draw their own cornucopia filled with emotions. Suggest they may represent their feelings in any way they please; they may utilize color and shape to represent the emotions.

Discussion/Goals:

Discussion focuses on the artwork, the amount and intensity of the feelings, and the way in which the client identifies with them. Goals include self-awareness, creative expression, and exploration of the connection between emotions, attitude and behavior.

Create a Friend

Materials:

Drawing paper, markers, crayons, pastels.

Procedure:

Suggest that clients design their ideal friend. Encourage them to think about the qualities this person would possess as they draw his/her features, hair, expression and overall style.

Discussion/Goals:

Discussion focuses on the figure formed, and examination of characteristics clients look for in a friend. Goals include exploration of relationships and connections in one's life.

Bridge to Happiness

Materials:

Drawing paper, markers, crayons, pastels.

Procedure:

Direct clients to draw a bridge that leads to bliss. Ask group members to specify through their drawing what type of joy they would discover at the end of the bridge.

Discussion/Goals:

Discussion focuses on what type of bridge was drawn (plain, fancy, strong, weak, long, short, colorful, etc.) and the happiness found at the end of it. Explore how it would feel to cross the bridge, how long would it take, and how the client would cross it (by foot, bicycle, car, etc.?). Examine the steadiness of it; possible bumps, potholes on it, etc. Use this exercise to help individuals identify goals and sources of contentment.

"It Is What It Is"

Materials:
Drawing paper, markers, crayons, pastels.

Procedure:
Discuss the meaning of this phrase and then ask clients to draw life as it is right now. Instruct them to use figures, shapes, abstractions, etc. to represent their thoughts.

Discussion/Goals:
Discussion focuses on exploring one's present life circumstances and feelings about it. Goals include acceptance, alleviating blame, and examining ways to cope with attitudes, emotions, daily issues and concerns.

Association[13]

Materials:
Drawing paper, markers, crayons, pastels.

Procedure:
Direct clients to draw an object associated with a significant event in their lives.

Discussion/Goals:
Discuss the significance of the object drawn and how it related to one's circumstances at the time. Goals include identification of feelings and self-awareness.

Billboard

Materials:
Drawing paper, markers, crayons, pastels.

Procedure:
Direct clients to create a billboard that advertises their attributes in some way.

Discussion/Goals:
Discussion focuses on the billboard and the message presented. Goals include increased self-esteem and identification of strengths.

The Window[14]

Materials:

Drawing paper, markers, crayons, pastels.

Procedure:

Ask clients to draw a large window and to include what they ideally would like to see when they peer out of it.

Discussion/Goals:

Discussion focuses on what was drawn (e.g. scenery, objects, people, fantasy scenes, etc.) and the client's reaction to his/her illustration. Goals include exploration of wishes and goals.

Draw Gratitude

Materials:

Drawing paper, markers, crayons, pastels.

Procedure:

Instruct clients to draw gratitude as a concept, or to represent it by drawing people, things, feelings, etc. they're grateful to experience and have in their life.

Discussion/Goals:

Discussion focuses on the meaningful things in the client's life and the ways in which she shows her appreciation. Goals include focusing on the positive, improving one's attitude and practicing optimism.

Transportation

Materials:

Drawing paper, markers, crayons, pastels.

Procedure:

Have clients choose from the list below and draw the type of transportation that expresses how they are currently feeling.

Race car, dog sled, elevator/escalator, pirate ship, tank, walking, yacht, 18-wheeler truck, ark, bike, train, camel, horse, canoe, helicopter, jeep, convertible, SUV, station wagon, van, jet, fire engine, ferry, garbage truck, taxi, camper, hot air balloon, battleship, chariot, surfboard, ice/roller skates, police car, rocket, motorcycle, subway, bus, trolley.

Discussion/Goals:

Discussion focuses on the mode of transportation chosen and the way it relates to the client's life, as well as physical and emotional state. Goals include introspection and self-awareness.

A Typical Day

Materials:

Drawing paper, markers, crayons, pastels.

Procedure:

Have clients outline a circle or provide one already outlined. Divide it into four squares labeled morning, afternoon, late afternoon and evening. Ask clients to sketch small figures (stick figures are fine) and represent what they do during different periods of the day.

Discussion/Goals:

Discussion focuses on the activities illustrated. Goals include assessing life satisfaction, and increasing awareness about leisure skills, specifically the importance of joining groups, socializing, and having hobbies and interests.

Draw Your Opinion of Yourself

Materials:

Drawing paper, markers, crayons, pastels.

Procedure:

Direct clients to draw their opinion of themselves. Tell them they may use shapes, abstract designs, lines, stick figures or life-like figures, etc.

Discussion/Goals:

Discussion focuses on the illustration and how it relates to self-esteem issues. Goals include attaining a realistic assessment of strengths and weaknesses. Clients often benefit from getting feedback from others because they frequently devalue themselves.

Addiction[15]

Materials:

Drawing paper, markers, crayons, pastels.

Procedure:

Instruct clients to fold their paper in half. On one side of the paper ask them to draw their "addictive personality" and on the other side have them draw their "normal or non-addictive personality."

Discussion / Goals:

Discussion focuses on observing similarities and differences between the personalities. Clients are encouraged to identify symbols in their artwork that serve as triggers for addictive behavior. They are supported to explore healthier and more appropriate outlets to feel content, fulfilled and less stressed.

A client named Kevin expressed conflict by drawing his "addictive personality" as the devil and his "normal personality" as a little boy with Jesus (represented by a cross) standing behind him. He stated that he doesn't want to let the little boy go because then he would have to take on all the responsibility that goes with being an adult. He stated he didn't want to work nine to five every day, and although he desired a family he was terrified of such a major change in his lifestyle. He remarked that he doesn't want to keep holding on to "the devil part of himself" but it is difficult to let go. Kevin blamed his addiction on his abusive childhood. He uses this as an excuse to continue drinking and spending money frivolously.

Strength I

Materials:

Drawing paper, markers, crayons, pastels.

Procedure:

Instruct clients to draw themselves as an important, healthy and strong individual in any way they please.

Discussion / Goals:

Discussion focuses on exploring group members' strengths and unique characteristics. Have group members examine their artwork and connect it to their thoughts and feelings. Emphasis is on mindfulness, positive self-talk, increased self-esteem and the power of positive thinking.

Stress and Relaxation I

Materials:

Drawing paper, markers, crayons, pastels.

Procedure:

Direct clients to fold their paper in half. Have them draw "relaxation" or themselves relaxing on one side of the paper, and "stress" or a stressful situation on the other side of the page.

Discussion / Goals:

Discussion focuses on how clients view their artwork and relate it to their feelings, emotions and experiences. Factors that contribute to stress and methods to attain peace and calm will be explored.

Draw a Scene From a Movie

Materials:

Drawing paper, markers, crayons, pastels.

Procedure:

Have clients think of a scene from a movie that reflects their mood, characteristics, personality or experiences and ask them to illustrate it.

Discussion / Goals:

Discussion focuses on the artistic representation of the scene, the characters included, and ways in which the client relates to the movie scene and artwork.

Goals include identification of thoughts and feelings and increased self-awareness.

An elderly female client drew herself as Scarlett O'Hara from *Gone With The Wind*. She remarked that "in her day" the men flocked towards her and she loved all the attention. She drew Scarlett surrounded by male suitors and remarked that she had many suitors, but she chose her husband because he was very kind and handsome, and stood out from all the rest.

A young man named Tom, who was recovering from depression, drew himself as Harrison Ford in *Raiders of the Lost Ark*. He stated he wanted adventure and was interested in seeing the world and studying archeology. He admired Ford's determination and bravery. Tom saw himself as stuck in a boring job and was searching for a more fulfilling life.

Draw Yourself as an Amusement Park Ride

Materials:

Drawing paper, markers, crayons, pastels.

Procedure:

Present a list of rides (or clients can make up their own ride) and ask group members to choose one that they could relate to in terms of their personality and/or lifestyle. Have them illustrate it.

Discussion/Goals:

Discussion focuses on the ride chosen, how the client relates to it, and the way in which it is drawn. Encourage group members to explore various personality characteristics. Goals include self-awareness and identification of unique qualities and behaviors.

RIDES:

Ferris wheel, roller coaster, carousel, boat ride (small boats that go in a circle in shallow water), log flume, Splash Mountain at Disney World, Orlando, Florida; (sit in a seat that travels through a cave filled with joyful tunes and puppets, and eventually goes straight down a steep slide and splashes into the water), tea cup ride (gentle circular ride), centrifugal force ride (stand up and gravity keeps you standing as you go round and round in fast circles), bumper cars, swing ride (swing gradually gets higher and higher, and then tilts), parachute drop, whip (circular seat that goes in a circle, and at certain points the seat makes a quick, jerky turn), Haunted Mansion at Disney World, Orlando, Florida; (sit in a seat and the ride takes you on a tour of a "haunted" mansion), trolley ride (gentle ride on winding tracks).

Leisure Skills

Materials:

Drawing paper, markers, crayons, pastels.

Procedure:

Ask clients to fold their paper in thirds. On the first third of the paper ask them to draw a leisure activity they enjoyed in the past, on the second third of the page ask clients to draw a leisure activity they presently engage in, and on the last third of the paper suggest group members draw an activity they would like to engage in, in the future.

Discussion/Goals:

Discussion focuses on the activities drawn, the reasons they have been continued or given up, and the satisfaction derived from engaging in them. Goals include leisure awareness and stressing the importance of hobbies and interests as a way of keeping active and involved, increasing self-esteem, and finding a purpose in life.

Draw Yourself as a Musical Instrument[16]

Materials:

Drawing paper, markers, crayons, pastels.

Procedure:

List various instruments such as a guitar, piano, flute, drum, xylophone, cello, viola, organ, trombone, saxophone, harp, violin, tuba, clarinet and cymbals. Instruct clients to choose the instrument that they relate to the most in terms of their personality characteristics and have them draw it in an abstract manner. Encourage the use of colors and shapes to reflect the personality of the client as it relates to the instrument.

Discussion/Goals:

Discussion focuses on personality traits. Goals include self-awareness and introspection. Soothing music playing in the background would be a pleasant accompaniment to this exercise.

Magnification

Materials:

Drawing paper, crayons, pastels, markers.

Procedure:

Increase the size of an object, person, emotion or feeling by 50–100 percent and draw it. The image should have significance for the artist.

Discussion/Goals:

This project enables the client to get a close look at things that are important to him and/or things that are blown out of proportion. For instance, one client drew a large figure of his wife because they are extremely close; another client drew a huge mouth representing that sometimes "he puts his foot in his mouth." Goals include self-awareness and identification of thoughts and feelings.

Draw Your Badge

Materials:

Drawing paper, pastels, markers, crayons.

Procedure:

Discuss the different types of badges people wear, e.g. a policeman's badge, a hospital worker's badge, a detective's badge, etc. and explore the message that is sent when someone is wearing one. Ask group members to draw a badge that relays the message that they are special.

Discussion/Goals:

Discussion focuses on the way in which the artwork illustrates the uniqueness of the client. Goals include self-awareness and increased self-esteem.

A young woman in her mid twenties drew a round sun with a large smiling face as her badge. It represented her outgoing personality and hope for a brighter future. A male patient in his seventies drew a frowning face to symbolize his anger, which he has to control in a healthier manner. A patient in his early twenties drew a skull and crossbones as a symbol of his "addict days."

Adult/Child

Materials:

Drawing paper, pastels, markers, crayons.

Procedure:

Have clients fold their paper in half and draw themselves as an adult on one side of the paper and as a child on the other side.

Discussion/Goals:

Discussion focuses on the drawings (observe the size, shape, body type, face, positioning and emotions illustrated). Examine what the figures might be saying to each other. Discuss what wisdom and/or suggestions the adult might be sharing with the child. Invite clients to share what life was like as a child and what life is like now. Goals include exploration of various experiences, the impact childhood has had on the adult personality, and wisdom acquired over the years.

A client named Rose drew herself as a joyful, carefree child wearing a colorful dress with bright yellow buttons and red ribbons in her pony tails. Her adult self was illustrated as a short, heavy woman wearing a black and brown dress, and emotionless. She remarked that the carefree days of childhood are long gone. Rose said that the adult would tell the child to enjoy every minute of her life because time goes by too quickly. She gave thanks that her parents were loving and wonderful. The drawing helped her see the importance of keeping that child within her alive in order to feel pleasure again, learn, grow and reach out to others.

Internal/External (addiction)[17]

Materials:

Drawing paper, markers, crayons, pastels.

Procedure:

Suggest that clients fold their paper in half. Have them draw something internal (e.g. loneliness, boredom, anxiety), that triggers drinking, on one side of the page, and something external (e.g. drinking buddies, walking by a bar, going to a wild party, etc.), that triggers drinking, on the other side of the page.

Discussion/Goals:

Discussion focuses on the triggers illustrated and ways to minimize or avoid them. Goals include self-awareness and identifying obstacles to sobriety.

View of the World

Materials:

Drawing paper, markers, crayons, pastels.

Procedure:

Provide the outline of a circle or have clients draw their own. Ask group members to fill it in with pictures, figures and symbols that represent their view of the world.

Discussion/Goals:

Discussion focuses on the client's thoughts, attitudes, values, outlook and mood. Explore how group members view the world: Is it a happy place? Do they need to protect themselves from it? Do they trust others? Do they see the world as dangerous or helpful and supportive? Examine ways in which they could improve their own world (community, home life, work place) and their environment. Discuss how one's view of the world affects his/her attitude toward therapy and working towards health and recovery.

Worry Tree[18]

Materials:

Drawing paper, markers, crayons, pastels.

Procedure:

Ask clients to draw a tree or provide an outline of one. Suggest participants use a combination of symbols, figures, words and shapes to represent their worries and concerns. Have them place their symbolic concerns where leaves would normally grow on their tree.

Discussion/Goals:

Discuss the type of tree drawn; explore its height, width, root system, amount of leaves (worries), age, and stability. Is it standing straight up or leaning over? The client will soon observe that there is a relationship between the tree and himself. Goals include expression of problems, issues, concerns, fears, and ways to cope with them.

Role in the Family

Materials:

Drawing paper, markers, crayons, pastels.

Procedure:

Have clients draw their role in the family, or the label they were given, e.g. the artist, the "smart one," the athlete, the sloppy one, the shy one, the trouble maker, the leader, etc.

Discussion/Goals:

Discussion focuses on the client's role in his family, his attitude about that role, and the way in which his self-esteem was affected. Explore the impact the role may have on him as an adult. Goals include identification of feelings, and reasons for certain behaviors, attitudes and beliefs about oneself.

Design Your Own Island

Materials:

Drawing paper, markers, crayons and pastels.

Procedure:

Instruct clients to create their own private island. Suggest they include what they would like on it, e.g. huts, fruit trees, animals, clear blue pools, a waterfall, etc.

Discussion/Goals:

Discussion focuses on the type of island drawn; its location, the mood of the island (is it a relaxing place for instance), and the benefits of living in such a place. Goals include exploration of one's dream environment and the similarities and differences between it and one's present living situation. Explore methods to attain a desired home environment.

The Future

Materials:

Drawing paper, markers, crayons, pastels.

Procedure:

Have clients draw what "they are not ready for yet." For example: Having a baby, moving to an assisted living facility, going to college, getting married, being a grandmother, etc.

Discussion/Goals:

Discussion focuses on where clients are now emotionally, socially, physically and financially. Explore expectations, hopes and fears about the future. Objectives include goal planning and exploration of wants and needs.

The Wizard of Oz[19]

Materials:

Drawing paper, markers, crayons, pastels.

Procedure:

Review the story of The Wizard of Oz with group members. Discuss that Dorothy and her friends were traveling the perilous yellow brick road to try to reach the wizard so that he could grant them their wishes. The tin man wanted a heart, the scarecrow wanted a brain, the lion wanted courage and Dorothy wanted to go back home to Kansas. Ask group members to draw their own unique version of the yellow brick road, what they would encounter on it, and what gift they would ask the wizard to grant them.

Discussion/Goals:

Discussion focuses on the road the client creates, his/her wishes and desires, and the amount of work clients will put into achieving their objectives. Goals include self-awareness and identifying values and needs.

Draw a Part of the Body[20]

Materials:

Drawing paper, markers, crayons, pastels.

Procedure:

Direct clients to draw one part of their body in which they feel physical or emotional pain. Next have them circle the illustration with the most healing and soothing color they can find.

Discussion/Goals:

Discussion focuses on the pain illustrated and how it affects one's emotional and physical state. Explore the ways in which the clients attempted to soothe their pain through the use of color. Explain how representing pain artistically provides a sense of control, and often lessens it; clients don't have to "own it" so much. Goals include exploring methods to cope with discomfort by using a variety of creative and cognitive methods.

This client's husband died three years ago. She suffers from anxiety and depression, and has had a series of electroconvulsive therapy treatments to try to uplift her mood and help her function more appropriately. She draws a red heart with an arrow piercing it to represent "the sharp, terrible heart pain" she suffers daily because of her sorrow. She says it is a non-relenting stabbing pain. The patient says, "Nothing will help, but perhaps the red color will heal me some day."

Two clients who were having obsessive thoughts, which they found "painful and frustrating," focused on drawing swirls and scribbles on their foreheads with various colors to illustrate their thoughts going around in circles.

The Bench

Materials:

Drawing paper, markers, crayons, pastels.

Procedure:

Instruct clients to draw themselves sitting on a bench and include whom they would like to be sitting next to them.

Discussion/Goals:

Discussion focuses on the person selected and the importance of that individual to the client. Explore the positioning of the two figures and their relationship. Goals include exploration of significant others, interactions, friendships and communication with others.

Tug of War

Materials:

Drawing paper, markers, crayons, pastels.

Procedure:

Instruct clients to draw themselves and one other person engaging in a game of tug of war. Review the game: Two people each have one end of a rope and they both pull on the rope until one person is able to pull the other person towards him with his share of the rope. That person is the winner of the game. It involves a lot of pulling and exertion of much energy. The players both work hard to acquire the rope for themselves.

Discussion / Goals:

Examine the illustration, how hard the figures are working, and who, if anyone, won the game. Have clients relate their artwork to their interactions with others. Explore whether they sometimes feel they are experiencing such a game with peers and/or family members. Discuss other areas in their life where they may feel at odds with someone or something else. Goals include identifying conflicts and exploring methods to resolve them.

Colors and Personality

Materials:

Drawing paper, markers, crayons, pastels, paint.

Procedure:

Have clients fill in ten squares (they may be provided or clients may draw them) with red, green, blue, yellow, brown, purple, orange, black, white and gray paint, crayon or marker. Ask group members to write a mood or feeling that each color evokes in them near the color square. Finally have them choose their favorite color and create a picture with it that depicts an aspect of their personality.

Discussion / Goals:

Discussion focuses on colors, related feelings and personality traits. Goals include exploring one's identity and characteristics.

Parents

Materials:

Drawing paper, markers, crayons, pastels.

Procedure:

Instruct clients to draw one thing they associate with their mother (e.g. apple pie, a walk in the park, an apron, a warm smile, etc.) and one thing they associate with their father (or mother and father substitute).

Discussion/Goals:

Discussion focuses on the item chosen and its meaning for the client. Goals include exploration of family relationships and the impact they have had on the psychological state, self-esteem and life of the client.

Self-Praise

Materials:

Drawing paper, pastels, crayons, markers.

Procedure:

Briefly discuss self-praise and the importance of it in order to increase self-esteem and satisfaction with life. Ask clients to report the last time they "patted themselves on the back" for a job well done. Ask them to draw themselves patting themselves on the back or praising themselves in some way.

Discussion/Goals:

Discussion focuses on the self-praise illustrated and how the clients feel while viewing their drawings. Goals include increased self-esteem and focusing on strengths and a positive attitude.

Upside Down Self-Portrait

Materials:

Drawing paper, markers, pastels, crayons.

Procedure:

Suggest that clients draw a self-portrait where they begin at their feet (top of the paper) and work their way down to their head (bottom of the paper).

Discussion/Goals:

Discussion focuses on feelings about this topsy-turvy figure and the ease or difficulty of creating it. Explore the various parts of the body and how the clients relate to them. Examine what it feels like to be upside down. Ask if clients could relate the figure to their present life circumstances, which may seem disordered and confusing. Examine how to cope with life when it does not go according to plan.

This picture was drawn by a young woman named Amy who remarked, "I'm standing on my head." She remarked that she enjoyed drawing in this manner because it gave her freedom to express herself. Amy stated that her world is "crazy" right now and confused. "I feel like all the blood is rushing to my head."

She said the picture reminded her of doing yoga exercises; she mentioned that she used to practice yoga to relax and to think things out. Amy laughed that her feet were drawn too large. She stated that she always had feet that were big, but now she needs them "to balance."

A man in his eighties jokingly said that he liked how he looked better with his feet as his head. He stated that it was easier for him to represent himself upside down, because he could get a clearer look at his "real self."

Most clients enjoy this exercise because they find it less threatening than drawing themselves the usual way. They often feel freer to share thoughts about their bodies and their self-image.

Symbols of Group Members

Materials:

Drawing paper, markers, crayons, pastels.

Procedure:

Have clients draw one thing that symbolizes each member of the group, e.g. someone might have bright red hair, another person may have a wide, joyful smile, someone else might be wearing a bright red shirt, etc.

Discussion/Goals:

Discussion focuses on the symbols illustrated and the clients' reactions to them. Explore if the clients see themselves as others see them. Examine similarities and/or differences. Goals include socialization, making connections with peers, and self-awareness.

Wash Day/Changes

Materials:

Drawing paper, markers, crayons, pastels, scissors, masking tape.

Procedure:

Ask clients to think of things in their life that need to be "washed" (changed, tidied, cleaned up). Have them draw these things (e.g. relationship problems, job problems, etc.) and cut them out. Suggest that participants place a piece of masking tape on each item drawn. Then direct group members to draw a box on another sheet of paper, which will represent a washing machine. Ask group members to decide whether the items drawn will go into the washing machine (get cleaned up/worked out) or will be left out for future cleaning. Have clients place the items to be washed in the machine. The masking tape is used so clients can have the freedom to take the items out of the machine if desired.

Discussion/Goals:

Discussion focuses on identifying changes that need to be made in one's life and incentives to make them. Objectives include examination of goals, coping skills and the work involved to make transformations and attain goals.

Cognitive Distortions and Positive Thinking

Materials:

Markers, drawing paper, scissors, glue.

Procedure:

Work with clients to develop a list of distorted thinking phrases such as: "I always have to be correct, I'm not smart, I can't do anything right, I know I'll never get well, everyone has it easier than I do, I should lose weight, I am going to be a lonely old person." Next ask clients to choose one of the phrases and illustrate the opposite of the phrase on a sheet of drawing paper. For example, if a client chooses the phrase "Nothing I ever do is correct" he might draw symbols, figures or illustrations representing himself doing something perfectly right; a gold star might be one example of a symbol that would be appropriate to use.

Discussion/Goals:

Discussion focuses on the transformation of the negative saying to the positive picture and the client's reaction to it. Goals include examining cognitive distortions and discussing ways to think in a healthier, more positive and productive manner.

Self-Esteem I

Materials:

Drawing paper, markers, crayons, pastels.

Procedure:

Ask clients to sketch people who helped raise their self-esteem in the past and who presently help raise it.

Discussion/Goals:

Discussion focuses on the individuals illustrated and their relationship to the client. Goals include exploring self-esteem and its relevance and importance to healing.

Protection

Materials:

Drawing paper, markers, pastels, crayons.

Procedure:

Ask clients to illustrate the question "How could you protect yourself?" Give examples such as "staying away from unpleasant or 'toxic' people, pursuing hobbies and social groups so that you're not bored and lonely, taking your medications, etc."

Discussion/Goals:

Discussion focuses on the form of protection illustrated and exploration of how clients support and take care of themselves. Goals include encouraging independence and positive self-care.

June, a 64-year-old woman, drew herself in a large bubble, stating she wishes the bubble would keep her "safe, secure, healthy and without depression." She remarked, "Sometimes I would like to keep the outside world away, especially when I listen to all the awful news that is on television." June stated that she wishes she could give a bubble to other group members so that they would feel better too. After further discussion she remarked, "Maybe the bubble isn't the best idea because I didn't draw a way out of the bubble." June mentioned that perhaps it would increase her isolation and loneliness. She finally decided that a bubble with a zipper might be the answer. June stated she wants to feel safe, but she also wants to be with other people as much as possible; "They can also help protect me, especially my daughter." The drawings helped June begin to express her thoughts, to examine ways to keep healthy and safe, and to reflect on her options.

Family Members Combination

Materials:

     Drawing paper, markers, pastels, crayons.

Procedure:

     Instruct clients to create a character that has at least one characteristic of each family member (or close friends). For example, the figure may have "your mother's eyes, and your father's nose, your sister's smile and your aunt's teeth." Group members may use as many family members as they please.

Discussion/Goals:

Discussion focuses on the figure created and his/her characteristics. Goals include defining the client's role in the family, exploration of family traits and how they affect family communication, relationships and dynamics.

Draw a Time (Recently or in the Past) That You Felt Joyful

Materials:

Drawing paper, markers, crayons, pastels.

Procedure:

Ask clients to draw a time in their life that they felt cheerful. Have them think of special people and events that had taken place. Encourage using colors that represent the positive feelings experienced at that time.

Discussion/Goals:

Discuss the drawing and focus on specific people, circumstances and/or the environment. Explore methods of attaining the happiness that was represented in the drawings.

Draw a Favorite Meal

Materials:

Drawing paper, crayons, markers.

Procedure:

Ask clients to think back over the years and draw a special meal that was cooked by them or someone else.

Discussion/Goals:

Discussion focuses on the meaning of food for each individual, and how one's eating habits can be representative of his mood and emotional state. Questions may include:

- How does food affect one's self-esteem and frame of mind?

- How does food assist a person in hiding from issues and uncomfortable feelings?

- What benefits are derived from eating comfort foods (potatoes, ice-cream, etc.)?

- Explore what food might represent to certain people (e.g. love, fulfillment, etc.)?

Draw Something You Are "Chained To"

Materials:
Drawing paper, markers, pastels, crayons.

Procedure:
Ask clients to draw something or someone they are "chained to."

Discussion / Goals:
Discussion focuses on the size, length and strength of the chain, and who or what the client is attached to. Goals include exploration of connections in one's life, boundaries, relationships and co-dependency issues.

Change II

Materials:
Drawing paper, markers, pastels, crayons.

Procedure:
Have clients fold their paper in half. On one side of the paper ask them to draw something that has remained steady for a long period of time and on the other side have them draw something that has recently changed.

Discussion / Goals:
Explore themes of safety and risk, and how clients react and adjust to change in their life. Goals include helping individuals to understand and accept that change is inevitable and they have the ability to control their reaction and attitude towards it.

Notes

1. This project would be better suited to clients who are comfortable with others and who do not have a thought disorder.

2. Under the Tools menu in many graphical applications you will see "Auto shapes." Under this category there are circles, squares, ovals, etc. Combining lines and shapes can easily create a stick figure.

3. This exercise is particularly beneficial to senior clients who derive a sense of self-worth and pride while reviewing their experiences and accomplishments. This is especially true when previous jobs, children and grandchildren are portrayed in their work.

4. This project may also be presented with collage materials, clay and/or paint.

5. This project was modified by a suggestion given to the author by Maggie Rusciano, RN, and Jill Gardner, ATR-BC.

6. This project is very beneficial to the senior population; it allows them to review events that may have been forgotten or repressed.

7. This project is very beneficial to the senior population: It allows them to review events that may have been forgotten or repressed.

8. This project is suitable for most adult populations, but it is especially satisfying for the senior community.

9. This is a modified version of an exercise suggested by Jill Gardner, ATR-BC.

10. This project is very helpful when clients are moving into a new home, especially if they are downsizing, as in the case of many seniors. It helps them feel better and in more control about what they take and what they leave behind. It is crucial for them to make their own choices and to be in charge of the move as much as possible.

11. Quote from "Poppy," in a presentation written by Linda Flower, LCSW at the 2008 NJAMC/NJAADA Conference at Rider University, New Jersey.

12. During a discussion, Adam Buchalter, BA, New York University, mentioned that he had a "cornucopia of feelings" after he broke up with his girlfriend. This thought was the basis for this directive.

13. Jennifer L.B. Katz, esq., suggested this directive.

14. This project has proven to be very successful with clients. It began as a warm-up but group members consistently chose to draw and focus on the symbolism for longer periods of time. Clients appear to enjoy the design and structure of outlining a window and including what they see out of it. A group of seniors who recently participated in this exercise drew a variety of thought-provoking illustrations including a city scene (because she wanted more stimulation in her life), children, grandchildren coming to visit, money, a beautiful beach and the return of a deceased loved one.

15. This project is particularly useful when working with addicts and individuals with obsessive-compulsive disorder.

16. This exercise was modified from an idea presented by Jennifer L.B. Katz, esq., 2008.

17. This project can be useful for all types of addictions including food and gambling addiction. The exercise can be generalized for use with anxiety and depressive disorders.

18. Other types of trees to use for this exercise may include a decision tree, a family tree, a leisure skills tree, a happiness tree and a goal-planning tree.

19. Modified from an idea suggested by Jennifer L.B. Katz, esq.

20. Senior clients often enjoy this exercise very much. It provides a sense of release for them, as well as camaraderie, since most clients are suffering some sort of pain.

CHAPTER 4

Painting

Painting allows for spontaneity and freedom. It is a medium that gives clients the ability to experiment with color, style and movement. Paint is particularly useful with clients who need to break free from rigidity and structure. It allows for flexibility, and flow in artwork.

Watercolors may be easier to work with for some clients. Clients maintain artistic control because they determine how dark or light, thin or thick the paint will be by adding more or less water to the mixture. It is a type of paint that is generally not too messy, easier to clean up, and can be painted over a pre-drawn outline. The watercolors that come in cases are contained and straightforward to manipulate.

Acrylics take a little more skill, but the colors can more easily be blended and mixed to form new shades. Individuals may use these paints to create abstracts or their own creative designs. They are easier to use and quicker to dry than oil paints.

There are paints that come in thick marker-like pens that can be dabbed onto the paper. These are very non-threatening, fun and simple. They can be used to create a variety of designs, including dot abstracts. Finger paints can be used for clients who are ready to express themselves freely. Finger painting to music is a favorite exercise of many clients who are ready to be messy "for art's sake." It is a pleasurable and imaginative exercise that allows the client to express himself through movement and art, and allows him to change his mind as many times as he pleases. Other painting techniques include sponge painting, painting with a mini roller, painting by blowing through a straw, marble painting, and using the brush to flick the paint on the paper like Jackson Pollock (to be worked on in a very structured environment with high functioning clients).

I suggest using non-toxic and washable paints; clients can become upset if their clothes become dirty or if they have difficulty cleaning their hands. As with other mediums, it is important to determine if the population you are working with will benefit from and be focused enough to engage in this medium.

Individual Mood Scale, Part I

Materials:

Acrylic paints, brushes, water containers, paint cups, paper towels, 12"×18" paper, pencils.

Procedure:

On the left side of the paper, ask group members to write the numbers 10 to 1 in descending order in a column (vertically). Then ask them to think of the numbers as a mood scale where their most positive mood is a 10 and their most negative mood is a 1. Direct clients to choose or mix a color which will correspond with the number on their mood scale, and place a small swatch of paint next to the number that corresponds to their particular need. On the remainder of the paper, suggest clients think about their present mood and create a piece of art using the colors and numbers that match how they feel.

Discussion/Goals:

Discussion focuses on examining how group members associate feelings to color and how various colors may relate to a wide range of moods. The manner in which clients use line, shape, color and design to represent mood may be examined. Goals include self-awareness, and expression of feelings.

Individual Mood Scale, Part II: Reviewing Progress

Materials:

Acrylic paints, brushes, water containers, paint cups, paper towels, 12"×18" paper, pencils.

Procedure:

Use the mood scales created in Part I and ask group members to fold their paper in half. Suggest they create a diptych using two colors that express how they felt when they started the hospital program (left); and how they are feeling now (right).

Discussion/Goals:

Discussion focuses on the use of color to assess progression, stagnation or regression in therapy. Procedures to attain therapeutic objectives may be explored. Goals include self-awareness, insight and acknowledgment of achievements.

Control II

Materials:

Watercolor pencils and paint (I prefer to use watercolors for this task), brushes, water containers, paint cups, paper towels, 12"×18" paper, pencils.

Procedure:

Ask clients to fold their paper into four sections. In each section, suggest they create an image showing one type of "control." Each square will illustrate what control means to them. Inform clients that "paint is a medium that allows for many different degrees of control." Suggest they use the medium itself to represent control, or they may create very specific and personal images.

Discussion/Goals:

Discussion focuses on exploring how clients depicted control, and the ways in which they are able to connect their images to feelings and attitudes about the amount and type of control they have. Goals include examining methods to gain better command of one's life.

Personal Flags

Materials:

Rulers, pencils, acrylic paint, brushes, water containers, paint cups, paper towels. A reference book that contains the flags of the world may be utilized.

Procedure:

Focus on how flags may represent individuals who belong to a specific country, community or culture. Explore various cultures and traditions that patients feel connected with and include social/spiritual groups, special organizations, etc. Suggest that each client list the group/s that he/she feels associated with and any symbols associated with that particular group. Have patients combine some of these symbols to create a personal flag.

Discussion/Goals:

Discussion focuses on formulating a personal and community identity. Goals include self-awareness, enhancement of communication, tolerance among cultures, and increased self-esteem.

Boundaries[1]

Materials:

Any type of paint should work for this task. Brushes, water, paint cups, paper towels, 12"x18" paper.

Procedure:

Ask clients to fold a piece of paper in half and instruct them to use it to create a piece of art that demonstrates equal balance (painting on both sides of the page). Tell them to then fold another sheet of paper in half and ask them to create a piece of art that demonstrates the give and take in a special relationship.

Discussion/Goals:

Clients are encouraged to compare their artwork to the distribution of balance in a current relationship. The task may provide a forum for discussing methods of maintaining healthy boundaries in relationships.

Totem Pole[2]

Materials:

It may be helpful to research information about totem poles and totem animals, and provide a handout (if you feel your clients will benefit from examples). The Internet has many examples of totem poles to use as samples. Pencils, acrylic paints, brushes, paper towels, 9"×12" paper, card or construction paper in a variety of colors.

Procedure:

Describe a totem pole: "a wooden structure created by Native Americans (and other cultures) to act as a symbol of a clan, tribe, family and its members." Have clients share totem pole images they have seen in museums, on trips, or in books. Suggest they try to describe totem pole animals they may have observed. Ask clients to create a group totem pole by having each client create an image of an animal that they feel represents them in character. Support them to join the pieces of art together and give the totem pole a name agreed upon by everyone.

Discussion/Goals:

Discussion focuses on each member's contribution to the totem pole, the animal chosen to represent the client, and the totem pole as a whole. Group dynamics may be explored by examining the positioning of the animals from top to bottom. Goals include group cohesion and unity.

Feedback

Materials:
Paint, water, brushes, paper towels.

Procedure:
Instruct clients to use lines, shapes and colors to express their feelings about giving or receiving feedback.

Discussion:
Healthy and effective methods of giving and receiving feedback may be examined by using the paintings as a way to stimulate conversation and insight into group members' communication styles.

Scratching at the Surface[3]

Materials:
Acrylic paints, water, brushes, paper towels, paint cups, paper.

Procedure:
Ask group members to cover their sheet of paper with a thin coat of paint, just thick enough so that the paper does not show through. Then using the tip of the paintbrush handle instruct clients to try scratching lines (zigzags, waves, criss-crosses) and shapes into the paint.

Discussion / Goals:
Discussion focuses on how group members felt while scratching into the paint, and then connecting their creative experience to the phrase "scratching at the surface." Encourage clients to explore what issues they are starting to "scratch at the surface" and how it feels to begin sharing problems and concerns with others.

Masking Out and Splattering[4]

Materials:
Painter's tape that can be easily removed from the paper you provide, acrylic paints, water, brushes, paper towels, paint cups, paper.

Procedure:
Instruct the group members to mask out a portion of their paper in any way they wish. Then using a paintbrush and colors of their choosing suggest they splatter

paint onto their paper. After the clients have finished painting have them carefully remove the tape from their papers.

Discussion/Goals:

Discussion focuses on how clients felt while splatter painting and how this painting approach might symbolize the way they are feeling and/or approaching issues in their life. For instance, are they scattered and not focused? Do they feel that they need more control in their life or do they yearn for the freedom felt while scattering the paint? Impulse control, organization, lifestyle choices and focusing may be addressed.

Paint Flicking[5]

Materials:

Tempera paints or acrylics, paper, brushes, water, cardboard box, toothbrush, stick.

Procedure:

Cut out the top and one side of an old cardboard box to make a screen that will keep surrounding areas clean, and lay paper on the bottom of it. Have clients flick paint onto the paper to create various patterns using an old toothbrush or a paintbrush. Clients can also strike the paintbrush against a stick to flick paint onto the paper. When the painting is completed ask clients to title it.

Discussion/Goals:

Discussion focuses on feelings that arise during the process of applying the paint (were individuals comfortable doing this; did they feel a sense of freedom; did they feel in control?). Explore the title of the painting and how the design relates to the mood of the artist.

Elements of a "Goodbye"[6]

Materials:

Paints, 18"×24" paper, brushes, water containers, paper towels.

Procedure:

Divide the group into pairs. Each pair of clients will share one sheet of paper. On the two outer sections of the paper, have each person paint lines, shapes and colors to represent the important elements of a goodbye. Then in the center section have each pair of clients create a more specific picture that depicts their thoughts. Ideally the two outer parts of the paper will be abstract, and the center part of the paper will contain a more structured illustration.

Discussion / Goals:

When a client is planning to leave a psychiatric program, is moving, or bidding farewell to friends, associates and/or family members it is helpful to explore the feelings that arise. This project helps clients better understand and deal with their troublesome and sometimes conflicting feelings. Goals include exploring satisfying, healthy and appropriate methods of ending relationships, and making connections with others.

Tea Time

Materials:

Paints, 18"×24" paper, brushes, water containers, paper towels.

Procedure:

Instruct group members to paint a scene of everyone sitting around a table drinking tea. Suggest that they create "conversation bubbles" above each person and write what each client might be saying in the bubbles.

Discussion / Goals:

Discussion focuses on perceptions about taking time to relax and socialize in the company of others. Group dynamics may be explored through the artwork and associated references. Goals include socialization and communication with others.

Art and Medications

Materials:

Watercolor paints, acrylic paints, water containers, brushes, paint cups, paper towels.

Procedure:

Ask group members to create a painting that represents their attitude toward taking medications. Encourage clients to visualize the size, color and shape of their medications. Suggest they incorporate into the artwork:

1. the way the medications make them feel (relaxed, anxious, angry, tired, etc.)

2. how the medications look and feel (large pills, tiny, smooth, coarse, chalky)

3. the way in which they take the medicine (does someone give it to them, do they take it at meals, first thing in the morning, with a lot of water, etc.)

4. the benefits and side effects of the medications.

When the painting is complete direct clients to title their work.

Discussion / Goals:

The majority of individuals in art therapy groups at the University Medical Center at Princeton are prescribed a variety of medications that manage psychological, emotional and physical symptoms. A strong negative response may be elicited when clients are instructed to take these medications. Painting helps clients express, accept and deal with their conflicting and negative feelings about taking medications.

Color Mood Pyramid

Materials:

Paper, assorted paints.

Procedure:

The therapist provides a large triangle (pyramid) on a sheet of paper and asks clients to fill the pyramid in with colors that represent their various moods. Clients are asked to begin at the bottom of the pyramid and build their color repertoire up, progressing from colors that represent sad or negative moods to colors that represent more positive moods. The top of the pyramid will contain the most positive color and brightest mood. A second sheet of paper with a pyramid on it should be distributed when clients are finished painting, and before the discussion takes place.

Discussion / Goals:

Discussion focuses on the various moods and colors associated with them. Explore behaviors and actions which may be connected to one's moods. Explore whether clients want to keep their mood pyramid in the order they were asked to draw it or if they choose to change the order. Have another pyramid outline available for possible changes. For instance, a client may feel that his positive feelings should be at the bottom of the pyramid, not the top. Goals include self-awareness and exploration of attitudes, feelings and personality characteristics.

Notes

1. Using paper that is folded down the middle provides a structure for patients to explore different levels of equality and balance.

2. A variation of this can be done using clay, wooden dowels or plaques that can be stacked.

3. This exercise would be best suited to clients who are recovering from depression and anxiety disorders, and who do not have cutting issues or suicidal ideation.

4. This exercise is best used with higher functioning clients since it can become an avenue for regression in some bipolar, schizophrenic, and immature clients.

5. This project would be suitable for clients who are able to maintain control and are functioning appropriately.

    For more ideas, visit www.Freekidcrafts.com and click *painting ideas*, then click *more painting ideas*.

6. This task is a modified version of an exercise was developed by Tracy Navarro in tandem with Susan G. Danielson, MS. Her inspiration was the concept of the "good-enough mother" introduced by Donald W. Winnicott (1988).

CHAPTER 5

Collages

Collage work allows clients to express themselves freely using a variety of resources. They are able to experiment with texture and touch, and to manipulate materials such as paper, photos, magazine pictures, fabric, foam shapes, felt, wood pieces, construction paper, pipe cleaners, cotton, etc. Collages may be presented in numerous ways. A theme may be presented, specific materials may be used, and the collage might be structured or non-structured. A structured approach might include having group members create a themed magazine collage such as an emotions collage by cutting out pictures of faces; a more non-structured approach might include having clients use a variety of materials such as wool and beads to represent inner feelings.

Individuals are often more willing to participate artistically when asked to design a magazine collage. This is partly because the pictures are easily accessible, there is not a right or wrong way to do this, and the photos just need to be torn or cut out. Clients have an array of ideas right in front of them. They can find photos representing their feelings, family members, hobbies, likes and dislikes, and just glue them on the paper in any way they please.

The collages are non-threatening ways of representing thoughts, concerns, attitudes and feelings. Clients usually feel free to share symbols represented in the collages. It is noteworthy to observe how the clients create their collages, whether they are full or empty, organized or disorganized, glued neatly or haphazardly. The therapist can observe fine motor skills by the way in which the client cuts and glues his pictures on the paper. The therapist gains knowledge about the way in which an individual approaches different types of creative clay work.

Beginning/End

Materials:

Construction paper, scissors, glue, markers.

Procedure:

Direct group members to create a collage using cut and torn paper shapes. Emphasize that the beginning and end of it should be clearly delineated.

Discussion/Goals:

Examine the collage and focus on its colors and forms. Explore the concept of beginning/end. Examine what it's like to complete a task, project, job, etc. from start to finish. Explore the meaning of perseverance and the importance of taking responsibility for one's own physical and mental health, and satisfaction with life.

Self-Esteem II

Materials:

Paper, pastels, crayons, markers, pencils, pens, construction paper, scissors.

Procedure:

The leader draws a wide variety of circular shapes on a sheet of white paper and Xeroxes it. Each group member receives a sheet and is asked to write a positive statement about himself/herself in at least four of the circles. Then clients are asked to decorate the circles, cut them out and paste them on a piece of construction paper (any color they wish) in order to create a pleasing design.

Discussion/Goals:

Discussion focuses on each individual's positive traits and the arrangement of the collage (e.g. Are there many circles included or only a few? Are the circles placed far apart? Do they overlap? Did the individual choose small circles or large ones? Are the circles drab or colorful? etc.). The ease and/or difficulty of sharing positive characteristics may be examined. Procedures to enhance self-esteem will be focused upon.

House Collage I: Ideal Home[1]

Materials:

Magazines, scissors, glue, paper, markers.

Procedure:

Direct clients to choose a variety of photos that represent their ideal home (dream home). Ask them to cut the photos out and glue them on the paper in any way they wish. Suggest they think about what makes a home special (people, pets, special belongings, etc.).

Discussion / Goals:

The relationship between one's home and one's personality may be discussed. Questions such as, "In what way does your home represent you?" can be asked. Suggest the client think about his/her home environment, belongings, color scheme, furniture or lack of it, degree of tidiness, etc. when pondering this question. Goals include exploration of methods to attain a more desirable home life, living space and environment.

House Collage II: Realistic Home

Materials:

Magazine photos, scissors, glue.

Procedure:

Provide the outline of a house that takes up most of a 9"×12" sheet of paper (or larger if desired). Direct clients to find pictures of things they have or had in their home, and instruct them to fill in the outline with these items. Hint that people and pets may be included.

Discussion / Goals:

Discussion focuses on exploring the clients' current living situation and satisfaction with their home life. Clients may compare the present reality of their living situation to their past reality (for instance, an elderly woman who wishes her husband was still with her may place the photo of a gray-haired man in her collage, or a client who lives modestly may include many luxury items in his collage to represent that he used to live in a larger home and was more financially secure). Goals include exploring how to cope with one's current situation and examining methods to accomplish realistic goals.

A client named Jan created a collage that was completely filled, with overlapping pictures of items of all sorts. She stated that her home was filled with television sets, computers, electronic gadgets, clothes, antiques and many other items that were costly and really unnecessary. She remarked that her home represented her need to collect things. She admitted she used objects as a source of pleasure and self-esteem "instead of people because people were too difficult to deal with."

Life Stages

Materials:

Magazines, scissors, glue, markers, paper.

Procedure:

Suggest that clients find photos from various magazines that represent different stages of their life and have them glue the pictures on a piece of 11"×14" paper in any manner they please.

Discussion/Goals:

Discussion focuses on examining how one's past affects present attitudes, beliefs and circumstances. Goals include increasing self-esteem and self-awareness by reminiscing about past experiences, achievements and strengths.

Laughter

Materials:

12"×18"paper, magazines, scissors, glue sticks, pencils.

Procedure:

Ask the group members to create a collage with the specific theme of laughter. The collage can be created by choosing magazine pictures of individuals laughing, and/or pictures that clients find humorous. Suggest that clients title their collage.

Discussion/Goals:

Creatively working with photos of people laughing offers clients a chance to reconnect with positive feelings. Group members may concentrate on how the face and mouth move when an individual laughs. Discussion focuses on how humor and laughter is beneficial to people physically and emotionally. Clients may be asked questions such as:

1.   What makes you laugh?

2.   When was the last time you laughed?

3.   How do you feel when you laugh?

4.   What was the last movie or television show that made you laugh?

5.   Who in your life makes you laugh?

6.   Explore how laughter lowers stress and anxiety and increases feelings of well-being.

Social Relationships

Materials:

12"×18"paper, magazines, scissors, glue sticks, pencils.

Procedure:

Group members will be asked to create a collage by collecting a number of magazine images that show two or more people interacting in some manner. Ask clients to title their collage.

Discussion:

Discussion focuses on exploring how people approach each other in order to develop connections and friendships. The therapist might point out that in magazine photos, as well as in other types of art and paintings, it is sometimes more common to observe individuals facing forward and smiling than it is to show individuals facing each other and interacting together. Explore how clients may or may not relate to this presentation and how they communicate with others. Relationship issues as well as boundary issues may be examined (standing too close, too far, etc.).

Patchwork Quilt Magazine Collage[2]

Materials:

Magazines, scissors, glue.

Procedure:

Instruct group members to cut small squares of fabric designs from magazines (approximately two or three inch squares). The designs may be cut from chairs, clothing, advertisements, etc. After a large amount of squares are cut out instruct clients to glue them on the paper in such a way that they resemble a patchwork quilt. Have them think about placement, color, texture and shape.

Discussion/Goals:

Discussion focuses on the pattern, colors and feelings evoked from the artwork. Goals include problem solving, enhancement of fine motor skills, focusing and concentration.

"Shout Out"

Materials:

Magazines, scissors, glue, colored construction paper, markers.

Procedure:

Have clients cut out words and photos from magazines that symbolize their hidden voice (what they want to say but haven't been ready or willing to share). Instruct them to choose a piece of colored paper that reflects their mood, and to place and then glue the words and photos on the paper in any way they please.

Discussion/Goals:

Discussion focuses on what clients desire to say and share. Goals include expression of thoughts, feelings, problems and concerns. One client remarked that she has very deep thoughts but doesn't know how to express them. This project provided the means to begin to share some of her pent-up feelings of anger and frustration.

My History

Materials:

Markers, crayons, pastels, drawing paper, magazines, glue, scissors.

Procedure:

Instruct clients to utilize photos from magazines and personal photos, if desired, to create a grouping of pictures that reflect various aspects of their life from youth to adulthood. They may also add words and illustrations.

Discussion/Goals:

Discussion focuses on life experiences and the role past experiences and relationships have on one's present mood, behavior and feelings. Goals include reminiscing and self-awareness.

Gift Basket

Materials:

Drawing or construction paper, markers, scissors, glue, magazines.

Procedure:

Ask clients to draw the outline of a large basket, or provide an outline. Have clients look through the magazines and find pictures of items they would like to have in their basket (may also include photos of people, animals and concepts such as happiness). Ask group members to glue the photos into and/or onto the basket in any way they please.

Discussion/Goals:

Discussion focuses on the items placed in the basket and the significance of the items. Explore the importance of the objects. Goals include identification of values, wants and needs.

Healing Collage[3]

Materials:

Construction paper, glue, scissors, magazines, assorted small items such as Band-Aids, smiling face stickers, a packet of hot chocolate, etc., that aid in healing and comfort.

Procedure:

Tell clients that they will be creating a healing collage, and they will begin to prepare for it.

- Direct them to write a variety of affirmations and positive statements on a sheet of paper, using large lettering and spaced far apart, so that the sentences may be cut out.

- Then ask group members to trace their hands, and write their name on the hand outlines. They may create a design on the outlines if they choose.

- The therapist will then make enough copies of the sayings and the outlined hands so that each client will have the opportunity to cut around the outlines and use them in his collage if he desires.

- Place the affirmations and handprints in the center of the table.

- Next tell clients they may use magazine pictures, the affirmations, the hand outlines, and assorted items presented or brought from home to create a healing collage. Magazine photos might include items such as people hugging or laughing, baby pictures, hot chicken soup, anything that the client views as a healing symbol. In addition they may glue other images and items on the collage, such as personal photos, a tea bag (representing comfort), the assorted positive sayings, and the outline of another group member's hand (comfort).

Discussion/Goals:

Discussion focuses on the reasons specific collage materials were utilized and the clients' feelings about the completed artwork. Goals include identification of needs, and exploration of ways to gain support, heal and become more content and functional.

Self-Care

Materials:

Construction paper, markers, scissors, glue, magazines.

Procedure:

Instruct clients to search for photos that represent ways in which individuals take care of themselves, and then glue them onto a sheet of construction paper in an appealing manner. Suggest they may look for photos of food, people exercising, eating in a healthy manner, bicycle riding, cooking, etc.

Discussion/Goals:

Discussion focuses on the design of the collage and the ways in which the clients relate to the photos chosen. Goals include exploring ways to maintain positive physical and emotional health, and identifying healthy lifestyles.

Stress II

Materials:

Construction paper, markers, scissors, glue, magazines, various decorative pipe cleaners, felt, foam, feathers, buttons, assorted collage materials.

Procedure:

Group members choose two sheets of colored paper that most closely represent stress to them (red and black are often chosen). One of the sheets is placed on the table and the other sheet is held. Suggest that participants tear the sheet of paper they are holding according to how much stress they are presently feeling. If they are not stressed they won't tear it; if they are a little stressed they will tear it in half; as the stress worsens they will tear the paper in more and more pieces. Clients may also crumble the paper if they wish to do so. After the sheets are torn and/or crumbled ask clients to glue them on the other sheet of paper in order to create a stress design. Tell them they may add the other materials provided.

Discussion/Goals:

Discussion focuses on the meaning of the collage and the focal point, which is the original pieces of torn paper. Explore how many times the paper was torn or crumbled, and what that means for the client. Goals include identification and expression of stress and anxiety, and exploration of coping mechanisms.

Abstract Drawing Collage

Materials:

Drawing paper or oak tag (thin cardboard), 18"×24" construction paper, markers, crayons, pastels, oil pastels, scissors, glue.

Procedure:

Instruct clients to create an abstract drawing using line, shape and color. Next have them cut the design into six to ten pieces, or more if desired. Have participants rearrange and then glue the shapes on the construction paper in order to form a collage.

Discussion/Goals:

Discussion focuses on the transformation of the original image to the new design. The theme of change may be explored. Goals include problem solving, focusing and enhancement of abstract thinking.

Notes

1   The house frequently symbolizes the body in literature and in dreams

2.   This project may be presented as an individual project or as a group mural where communication, teamwork, cooperation and socialization would be the main goals of the session.

3.   This project may be divided into two sessions if desired because there are a number of steps involved.

CHAPTER 6

Clay

Clay work promotes expression of mood and feeling. It allows the clients to experiment with texture and touch by molding, shaping and manipulating the clay. Pounding and kneading the clay offers a healthy way to exert excess energy. Gently molding, stroking and smoothing it lessens stress and anxiety. Clay provides a way to turn an amorphous shape into something specific. In a few minutes a ball can be transformed into a tiny pinch pot by placing and then pressing one's thumb in the center of it. There are numerous projects that can be designed. Some of these include pots, trays, figures, animals, abstract designs, family sculptures and masks. The ease or difficulty of the projects will depend on the population one is working with.

There are many different types of clay that may be used. Terracotta is suitable for many types of work and can be fired. Some clients don't like it because it is messy and dries the hands. Other clays include *Sculpey, Crayola,* home-made clay (recipes can easily be found on the Internet) and *Model Magic Clay.* Model Magic is a favorite among clients because it is clean, non-toxic, air dries, and is easily used.[1]

Clay affords the client the opportunity of working three dimensionally, seeing things from more than one perspective. The individual becomes the master of the clay; he is in control of it. Utilizing clay allows clients to mold behaviors, attitudes and self-image. Participants gain insights and develop new methods of coping and problem solving.

Worry Stones

Materials:

Non-toxic clay, such as Sculpey (can be bought in most art supply stores or purchased online) or polymer clay (this clay is not powdery or dusty and remains workable until baked; it can be baked in the home oven), index cards, plastic knife, tray.

Procedure:

Share with clients that worry stones are of ancient Greek origin; rubbing was believed to lessen worry. Have group members choose three different colors and have them cut three marble sized pieces of the clay or have the clay cut beforehand. Ask clients to squish the colors together and twist the clay a few times. Have them create a sphere and place it on the index card. Ask clients to press their thumb down into the clay to form a bowl shape; the bottom will be flattened. As they press down suggest that the edges surrounding the hollow should be smoothed and moulded into a type of mini tray. Ask them to etch their initials into the bottom of the clay gently and place the clay back on the index card. Clients can take the clay home and bake it themselves or the leader can bake the pieces and distribute back to clients.

Discussion/Goals:

Discussion focuses on the stones' healing qualities and the importance of keeping a positive outlook. Self-soothing, calming techniques are explored. Having a tangible object that can be used for healing is very therapeutic.

Family Scene I

Materials:

Any type of clay available (terracotta clay works well), 12"×18" sheet of drawing paper, markers, crayons, pastels.

Procedure:

Direct group members to create figures that represent family members. Emphasize that the figures do not have to look realistic. Clients may create as many figures as they please but, if possible, the minimum should be two individuals. When the figures are completed ask that they be placed on a large sheet of paper, perhaps 12"×18". Suggest that clients draw an environment around the figures, e.g. a living room, park, the beach, etc.

Discussion/Goals:

Discussion focuses on the figures chosen (mother, father, aunt, etc.) and the reasons these individuals were chosen. Explore their placement on the paper, their relation to one another (for instance is the client placed near the mother, apart from the father?), and their size. Family members left out of the scene might also be examined. Goals include self-awareness, becoming conscious of the effect that each person's family has on his/her self-esteem, emotional state, outlook, and direction in therapy.

Size Differential

Materials:

Clay (modeling clay or air-drying clay is preferable for this task). Waxed paper, clay tools and Popsicle sticks can be offered, but are not necessary; water will be needed for air-drying clay.

Procedure:

Allow patients time to become accustomed to the clay. Suggest they squeeze, roll out, ball up the clay, and try to adjoin two pieces together. After this warm-up instruct group members to create two objects that are exactly the same except that one of the objects must be larger than the other.

Discussion/Goals:

Discussion focuses on the objects created (see if clients can associate the objects to people in their lives), the size difference (appreciably larger or slightly larger) and possible significance of the size difference. The therapist may question group members about the relationship between the two objects. Ask clients, "If these objects were able to speak to each other what would they say?" Highlight and discuss power relationships, nurturing relationships and related feelings. Goals include self-awareness and acknowledgment of one's role in pertinent relationships.

Group Fruit and Vegetable Basket

Materials:

Polymer clay in a variety of colors works well for this task: it is not powdery or dusty, remains workable until baked, and can be baked in the home oven; bowl or basket.

Procedure:

Ask clients to list different types of fruits and vegetables while visualizing their color, shape and texture, and imaging how they smell and feel to the touch.

Part I: Suggest that group members create a miniature-sized fruit or vegetable from the clay provided.

Part II: Direct them to place their fruit or vegetable with all the others in the bowl or basket.

Discussion/Goals:

Discussion focuses on the reason the specific fruit/vegetable was chosen and how the client may relate to the fruit and/or vegetable (e.g. sweet like a plum, sour like grapes). Mindfulness in terms of familiarizing oneself with the texture, color and scent of the fruit may be emphasized. Goals include socialization, making connections and working as a group to promote greater self-esteem.

Identity[2]

Materials:

Various types of clay.

Procedure:

Direct clients to create an object/figure (realistic or abstract) that "can represent you as a whole." The clients may be given a time frame depending on the session length. Once this task is completed, ask each group member to consider how he or she thinks mental illness (or other symptoms) affects him or her.

Next suggest that group members choose another piece of clay and create a symbol from it that represents their mental health symptoms. Finally, ask them to incorporate the second sculpture (mental health symptoms) into the first sculpture (self-representative object) so that the two pieces of clay form one sculpture.

Discussion/Goals:

Discussion focuses on identifying and discussing how group members view themselves, and exploring the ways in which stigma affects clients. Group members are supported to share their perspectives of mental illness and how it impacts identity. The idea that it does not have to take over identity is emphasized. Goals include increasing self-esteem and self-awareness.

Clay Mandala[3]

Materials:

Many types of clay work well for this project. Other materials needed include a rolling pin, water or spray bottle, waxed paper, a round cookie cutter, Popsicle sticks, shells, beads, stampers, buttons, beads, small wood pieces, sequins, pipe cleaners and any items that can be pushed into the clay to leave an impression.

Procedure:

"A different approach to mandala making." Introduce mandalas (circles used for focusing and healing) to the group. Discuss the aspects of a circular pattern, wholeness, unity, etc.

1. Clients are asked to experiment with the clay by molding, kneading and manipulating it.

2. Demonstrate how to create a flat circular cutout from the clay on a square of waxed paper: wedge clay and then roll it out using a rolling pin to ½ inch in thickness.

3. Depress the round cookie cutter into the clay.

4. Remove excess and save in a plastic bag.

5. Once each patient has a clay circle, they can choose how they would like to complete their mandala using other materials provided.

Discussion/Goals:

Ask clients to share how they felt creating the mandala and have them describe their design and/or pattern. Suggest they share the meaning of their work. Discuss whether there are any themes common among members of the group. Question how the creation of the mandala relates to focusing inward, and/or wholeness. Goals include self-awareness, focusing and expression of mood and feeling.

Brick Wall

Materials:

Clay (modeling clay or air-drying is preferable, water will be needed for air-drying clay). Task can be done with re-usable modeling clay or with air-drying clay.

Procedure:

Ask clients to describe what a brick wall can represent metaphorically or as a symbol. Offer each client a piece of clay and waxed paper to work on. Direct group members to create a brick wall by making blocks from the clay and then stacking them in some way. Next, ask clients to imagine what might be on the other side of the wall and have them create an object or symbol of what they visualize in clay.

Discussion/Goals:

Prompt a discussion about the relationship between the wall and the object/symbol that each client placed behind the wall. This task can be helpful in identifying what the client perceives as an obstacle (the wall) and what they desire on the other side. The task can also be used to prompt discussion of the wall as a necessary boundary to control their impulses or separate them from their past. The task can help the client share fears and aversions. It may be helpful to prompt a discussion about what types of brick walls were built.

Questions may include:

- What shape, height/width, etc. is the wall?
- Is it solid, or are there holes and gaps?
- Were large or small blocks used to create the wall? What is the significance of these features?
- How long has the wall been up?
- What is the size and strength of the wall?

Goals include becoming aware of and dealing with barriers to recovery.

Stone Wall

Materials:

Any type of pliable clay.

Procedure:

Instruct clients to form small balls out of the clay and connect them together to build a wall.

Discussion/Goals:

Explore the size and strength of the wall. Discuss ways in which the client may relate to the wall. Examine the use of walls (to keep things/people out or in) and have clients share the purpose of their individual walls. The balls are used so that it will be effortless for clients to break down parts of the wall if they choose to do so during the course of the discussion. Goals include exploration of obstacles to recovery and attaining goals.

The Mask and Behind the Mask[4]

Materials:

Clay, water or a spray bottle, waxed paper; clay tools can be offered, but are not necessary.

Procedure:

This task often takes on more meaning for clients when using clay than with pre-shaped masks, because they have more flexibility with the expressions and shapes of their masks. Clients can mold a head and face from clay and then mold and fit a mask to fit their face.

Provide patients with clay and waxed paper to work on. Ask them to split their clay in half and use one half to create a head in any manner they would like.

With the second half ask them to consider what type of mask may be appropriate for the head they created and to attempt to create this mask.

Discussion/Goals:

Discussion focuses on the head and mask created. Generally the client will relate the mask to the way he/she masks his/her feelings and the head to his/her true self. Discussion focuses on how masking feelings helps and/or hurts one's ability to share in therapy, acknowledge problems, strengths and weaknesses and relate to others. Questions to ask clients include:

- Is the head and/or mask self-representative?

- What feeling do you get when you look at your head/mask?

- Is the head/mask pleasing, frightening, sad, joyful, etc.?

- Is the mask similar or different to the head?

- Did you choose to place the mask on the head/face or leave it next to the head/face?

- Goals include exploring identity and barriers to interacting with others.

Variations can be done with other types of 3D masks and mask-making, or 2D materials.

Leaving the Past[5]

Materials:

Air-drying clay, rolling pins, a variety of beads, sequins, tiles, or any small objects that can be pressed into the clay.

Procedure:

Suggest that group members create a small clay mosaic that represents feelings and/or things in their past they would like to leave behind. Have the group wedge and then roll out their clay with the rolling pin (about ½ an inch in thickness seems to work well). Ask clients to choose a few of the small objects presented and press them into the clay to embed them.

Discussion/Goals:

Discussion focuses on the experience of embedding objects in clay, and the feelings related to leaving unpleasant thoughts and parts of one's past behind. Discuss what type of experiences and/or thoughts clients are burying. Goals include self-awareness, relief of tension and feeling a sense of control by symbolically burying feelings, issues and unpleasant memories. Question such as, "Is it wise? Is it effective to bury feelings and things from the past?" may be explored.

Clay Animation: A Comedy

Materials:

Modeling clay is all that is needed for this task, although clay tools, armature wire, a digital camera and a computer can also be utilized.

Procedure:

Ask group members to create a figure out of clay and to think of a humorous story they can tell by moving the parts of the figure in various ways.

Discussion/Goals:

Discussion focuses on what types of humor group members enjoy and what specifically makes them laugh. Encourage clients to explore how it feels to laugh and how it feels to make others laugh (for example, self-esteem is often raised). Explore the humor in the figure created, the way it was animated and in the story told. Share the therapeutic benefits of laughter (better mood, decreases stress, lowers blood pressure, increases socialization, etc.).

Self-Esteem III

Materials:

Terracotta or any type of clay desired.

Procedure:

Have clients mold shapes representing self-esteem, and place them in an chronological order reflecting changes in their self-esteem over the years.

Discussion/Goals:

Discussion focuses on the representations and how they symbolize feelings of self-worth and confidence. Observe similarities and/or differences in the shapes. Goals include assessment of self-esteem and the way it affects mood, actions and behavior.

Notes

1   These clays are easily manipulated and non-toxic. They may be easily found on the Internet, such as at Nasco, (www.enasco.com) or S&S Crafts (www.ssww.com), or in most art supply stores.

2   This is a complicated project so the therapist must carefully examine the amount of time he/she has as well as the clients' ability to focus and problem solve. It can be broken down, if need be, into a series of two to three sessions. This project has been successfully utilized with schizophrenic and bipolar clients, but it can be used with a variety of populations.

3.   If you have access to a kiln, earthenware clay is preferable. Pieces can be fired to bisque and glazed. Finished pieces can be used as coasters as well.

4.   Polymer clay in a variety of colors works well for this task, however it is not necessary. Home-made clays, modeling clay, air-drying clay or earthenware will work as well.

5.   Caution should be used when utilizing this task with unstable clients, or clients with trauma in their history. It should be clarified to clients that burying feelings and experiences can be beneficial if they are self-defeating, but the practice can also become a defense mechanism, and a way to hide from reaching out to others and sharing important concerns. Depressed clients who dwell on past mistakes and obsess over unrealistic worries and concerns would highly benefit from this exercise.

CHAPTER 7

Puppets and Masks

Designing puppets and masks enables clients to project their thoughts and feelings onto objects that can be viewed as self-representative. It is often easier and less threatening to express feelings when using a puppet or mask as a prop. Role-play is a significant benefit to engaging in these types of projective tasks. Clients may use the puppets and masks to speak for them; they may hide behind them in order to feel safer when sharing.

There are a large variety of puppets and masks that may be created. Masks may be made from materials such as clay, cardboard, foam, papier mache, aluminum foil, paper bags, paper plates, etc. Puppets can be designed from items such as clothespins, milk cartons, cardboard rolls, flowerpots, wool, newspaper, Styrofoam cups and burlap. The projects may be as complicated as marionette making or as simple as creating a puppet from the finger of a woolen glove. It depends on the population one is working with and the therapist's goal for the group session. Regardless of the complexity or simplicity of the project, play-acting with puppets and masks is an enjoyable creative experience that allows clients to explore inner feelings and outer experiences.

Flowerpot Figure

Materials:

Small flowerpots (4"–6"), glue gun and/or a very strong squeeze glue, 2"–3" Styrofoam balls, paint, glitter, wool, sequins, feathers, pipe cleaners, wiggle eyes, mini doll hats if available and any other tiny accessory available.

Procedure:

Inform group members that they will be creating a figure that should be self-representative in some way. Instruct clients to paint the flowerpot (the body) and the Styrofoam ball (the head) and let them dry. Then assist clients to glue the head on the body with the hot glue gun or other very strong glue. Clients may now add a face, hair, hat, arms (pipe cleaners) and any other decorative item they please.

Discussion / Goals:

Discussion focuses on the way the figure is designed and the way in which it is symbolic of the client. For example, one client created a cowboy-like person to represent his "wild ways." A female client designed "Groucho Marx" to represent her sense of humor. A woman named Lenora created a "Hollywood Star"; she designed her figure with red hair (feathers), sequins and glitter to represent "the importance of a good appearance." She stated that her appearance is what provided her self-esteem in the past and helped her get desired jobs and form positive relationships. Now that her looks were fading and she developed back problems she was finding she was becoming increasingly depressed and isolated.

Fly Swatter Puppet

Materials:

A cheap fly swatter (can be purchased in dollar stores), pipe cleaners, beads, sequins, wiggly eyes, buttons, pom poms, felt, wool, feathers and any other small decorations, glue, scissors.

Procedure:

Suggest that clients will be creating puppets in any way they please. Instruct them to glue on feathers (for hair), wiggly eyes, felt, etc., to create a person, animal or creature. A glue gun would be helpful but not necessary.

Discussion/Goals:

Discussion focuses on the type of person or creature designed and the ways in which it might be self-representative. Since the puppet is designed from a fly swatter, ask clients if they have anyone or anything in their life that they would like to swat. Goals include creative expression and expression of frustration and/or irritation.

Wooden Spoon Puppets[1]

Materials:

Wooden spoon, paint, feathers (for hair), wiggly eyes, glue, material, felt, etc. A glue gun would be helpful but not necessary.

Procedure:

Instruct clients to paint the spoon. The top of the spoon (the head) may be painted a different color, if desired, from the handle. When the spoon is dry have clients decorate it and transform it into a person. They may leave the handle as is or they may wrap material or felt around the handle and decorate it to create clothes.

Discussion/Goals:

Discussion focuses on the figure created and the meaning it has to the client. This type of puppet can be held by the handle (the body) so group members may manipulate it while they engage in role-play. They may ask the puppet questions, tell the puppet thoughts, and/or have the puppet speak to them. Goals include expression of thoughts and feelings, and sharing of issues and concerns.

Feather Duster Puppet

Materials:

Feather duster (can be found in dollar stores), feathers (for hair), wiggly eyes, material, felt, glue, etc. A glue gun would be helpful but not necessary.

Procedure:

Direct clients to glue decorative objects on the feathers to create a face.

Discussion/Goals:

Discussion focuses on the face designed and ways in which it is self-representative. The puppet is a feather duster so questions to ponder include, "What in your life would you like this puppet to dust away and how long ago did the dust (problems) begin accumulating?" Goals include identifying problems and concerns.

Finger Puppets

Materials:

Old gloves, feathers (for hair), wiggly eyes, ribbon, foam, scissors, yarn, material, felt, buttons, glue, etc. A glue gun would be helpful but not necessary.

Procedure:

Cut the fingers off the gloves and sew the base of the holes to prevent unraveling. Glue is fine to use too. Use wiggly eyes, ribbon, felt or tiny foam pieces for eyes; add a nose, a mouth and hair. The puppets may be dressed with fabric, felt, etc. Tiny felt hats might be designed, as well as tiny bows, scarves, etc.

Discussion/Goals:

Discussion focuses on the design of the puppets and role-play (if the clients are ready and willing for this exercise). Encourage clients to speak through the puppets and share thoughts and feelings. Clients may introduce themselves or share something about themselves they haven't shared before using the puppets as their props.

Cardboard Roll Puppets

Materials:

Paper towel rolls or toilet paper rolls, small Styrofoam balls, craft sticks, glue, scissors, construction paper, feathers (for hair), wiggly eyes, material, felt, glue, etc. A glue gun would be helpful but not necessary.

Procedure:

Suggest to clients that they may create one or more puppets that will represent family members in some way. Instruct them to glue the Styrofoam ball on the paper holder with a strong glue or glue gun, and let dry. Direct them to paint the roll and, if desired, also to paint the Styrofoam ball. Tell them to add various decorations to create a face, hair and clothes.

Pipe cleaners may be attached with the glue gun to create arms and legs.

Discussion/Goals:

Discussion focuses on the family members represented and the relationship the client has with them. Goals include exploration of family relationships and the client's role in his/her family.

Humorous Masks[2]

Materials:

Plastic eye masks, glue, scissors, sequins, glitter, buttons, feathers, pom poms and other accessories.

Procedure:

Instruct clients to create a mask that represents "the comedian in you."

Discussion/goals:

Discussion focuses on the humor represented in the mask. Ask clients to describe additional ways that they express their sense of humor. Explore the importance of humor in one's life and how it helps decreases stress, blood pressure and worries. Examine the benefits of laughter and explore things that clients find entertaining. Discuss how humor may be an effective coping mechanism; for instance, watching a comedy show often alleviates stress.

Collage Masks

Materials:

Cardboard or poster board, glue, scissors, sequins, feathers, buttons, felt, ribbon, yarn, paint, brushes, magazines, small boxes, string, foam pieces, tissue paper, and any other ornament or accessory suitable.

Procedure:

The therapist distributes pre-cut masks or cuts out a template of a mask in whatever shape she desires (circular, oval, square, etc.), which clients are asked to copy onto the cardboard and cut out. Eyes will need to be cut out before decorating. Instruct clients to paint the mask if they desire, and then to use whatever materials they please to create a mask that is unique.

Discussion/Goals:

Discussion focuses on the way the mask was designed and the media used. Choosing the materials and deciding on their placement requires much contemplation and effort. Higher functioning clients will benefit from role-play as a way to express feelings and emotions. Goals include freedom of expression, experimentation, decision making, and problem solving.

Papier Mache Masks

This technique was presented in *A Practical Art Therapy* (Buchalter 2004). Creating masks using papier mache provides an enjoyable and therapeutic learning experience for clients, therefore I wanted to include it in this chapter.

Materials:

Balloons, newspaper, paint, wool, feathers, collage materials.
For the papier mache paste: 3 cups flour (add a little more if too sticky), 1/3 cup salt, 2 tbsp vegetable oil, 1 cup water, 7 drops food coloring (if desired).

Procedure:

Mix the papier mache paste ingredients well. Have clients blow up a balloon and then cut or tear strips of newspaper, which they dip into papier mache paste. You may use store-bought paste or the recipe given in the note section. Instruct clients to place these strips on their balloon (about three quarters of the way around). Let the balloon dry for about 24 to 48 hours. When the balloons are dry, clients will break them with a pin and cut the hardened papier mache until it looks mask-like and covers the face. Clients may decorate the mask with paint, beads, wool, etc. When creating the face, individuals can add the nose, lips, chin, eyebrows, etc. by taking paper towels, soaking them in the papier mache paste and molding features on the face (in the same way as working with clay). Newspaper dipped in papier mache paste combined with strips of dry paper towels will facilitate the drying process.

Discussion/Goals:

Discussion may focus on the ease or difficulty of the technique used to create the mask, the way in which it is self-representative, its appearance and expression. Goals include exploration of feelings and self-image.

Aluminum Foil Masks[3]

Materials:

Aluminum foil, glue, scissors, feathers, wool, yarn, sequins, markers, buttons, and other accessories.

Procedure:

Cut two pieces of heavy aluminum foil, large enough to cover the client's face. Have the client place the foil over his face and press in so that the outline of his features becomes somewhat apparent. When he removes the foil have him gently place it on the table and round the edges carefully so it has a mask-like shape. Now suggest he decorate it in any way he pleases. The client may cut out holes for the eyes, but this is not necessary because it will be used as a decorative mask, not meant for clients to wear.

Discussion/Goals:

Discussion focuses on the character created and its relationship to the client. Goals include expression of feelings and abstract thinking.

Stick Masks

Materials:

Popsicle sticks, glue, scissors, tape, cardboard, magazines, templates.

Procedure:

Go to play.powerhousemuseum.com/makedo/pdfs/stick_mask.pdf. This web page offers a variety of facial features that can be cut out, glued on cardboard and made into masks by attaching a stick onto the cardboard. This type of mask can also be created using magazine photos of facial features, and then combining them to create a face.

Discussion/Goals:

Discussion focuses on the character formed, as well as thoughts and feelings related to it. Clients may try to associate their masks to aspects of themselves or people they know. Emotion, mood and feeling may be explored by examining the facial features.

The photos on the website are very striking; there are many exercises that can be presented utilizing them. For example, they may be used to create a collage of facial features, or clients might construct a face using the features provided.

Mardi Gras Masks

Materials:

Plastic eye masks or eye masks taken from a template (see note 2), feathers, sequins, pipe cleaners, glitter, scissors, glue, doilies, beads, buttons, felt, crepe paper, etc.

Procedure:

Provide the mask or template outline. If using the template outline, cut it out and glue it on the cardboard. Then cut the cardboard to fit the shape. Eyes may be cut out if desired. Glue the glitter, buttons, feathers and other decorations on it. A doily cut in half and glued to the back of the mask (arc shape) will create that special festive look. Finally attach a stick to the mask so it can be held up.

Discussion/Goals:

Explore the appearance of the masks and then talk about the enjoyment and festivities associated with Mardi Gras. Discuss the way in which clients allow themselves to have fun; explore parties, galas and parades clients have attended in the past. Questions to ask include: "Would it be helpful to hide behind masks at these events?" and "Would you act differently right now if you had this mask on?" Explore the benefits and negatives of wearing a mask. Goals include self-awareness and creative expression.

Notes

1. Role-play can be threatening, so it is important to assess whether or not the population you are working with is stable enough to engage in this creative exercise. Some clients may feel more comfortable talking about the appearance of their puppet and discussing how they felt designing it, rather than the way in which it is self-representative.

2. Plastic eye masks may be purchased in S&S Crafts (www.ssww.com) and are sometimes found in dollar stores and sometimes in art supply stores. If you would like to use cardboard or paper masks, a template can be printed from the Internet. Try going to FamilyCrafts.about.com/library/color/bleyemask.htm and type "eye mask template" into the search box.

3. Since the foil is briefly placed over the face, make sure the client is comfortable with this procedure, otherwise the therapist may place it on her face and allow the client to use that outline to complete his mask.

CHAPTER 8

Combining Modalities

Combining modalities such as poetry, music, movement, creative story writing and art provides a rich environment for creative expression and sharing of thoughts, ideas and feelings. Clients are given a variety of ways to communicate with others and share attitudes toward life, relationships and recovery. Poetry and art helps clients focus on problem solving and abstract thinking, while movement and art assists clients to get in touch with their bodily sensations and observe how their movements communicate emotional and physical issues. Creative writing and the use of metaphors afford individuals the opportunity to be mindful, to examine philosophies, and to find various ways to look at life, love and relationships. After reading a passage group members are asked to interpret and illustrate the meaning of what was written. The combination of the modalities adds excitement and energy to therapy groups. Clients gain greater insight and increase their abstract thinking. Black and white thinking (rigidity) transforms into colorful thinking (more flexible viewpoints).

"The Trapeze"[1]

Materials:

Paper, pastels, crayons, markers.

Procedure:

Read group members the following essay, and then ask them to draw themselves on a trapeze going from one bar to another.

> Sometimes I feel that my life is a series of trapeze swings. I'm either hanging on to a trapeze bar swinging alone, or for a few moments, I'm hurtling across space in between bars. Most of the time I'm hanging on for dear life to my trapeze bar of the moment. It carries me along at a certain steady rate of swing and I have the feeling that I'm in control of my life. I know most of the right questions and even some of the right answers. But once in a while as I'm merrily swinging along, I look ahead of me into the

distance and I see another bar swinging towards me. It's empty and I know, in that place in me that knows, that this new trapeze bar has my name on it. It is my next step, my growth, my aliveness coming to get me. In my heart-of-hearts I know that for me to grow, I must release my grip on the present, well-known bar to move to the new one.

Each time it happens, I hope and pray that I won't have to grab the new trapeze bar. But in my knowing place I realize that I must totally release my grasp on my old bar and for some time I must hurtle across space before I can grab onto the new bar. Each time I am filled with terror. It doesn't matter that in all my previous hurtles across the void of unknowing, I have always made it. Each time I am afraid I will miss—that I will be crushed on unseen rocks in the bottomless chasm between the bars. But I do it anyway. Perhaps this is the essence of what the mystics call the faith experience. No guarantees, no net, no insurance policy, but you do it anyway because, somehow, to keep hanging onto that old bar is no longer an alternative. And so for an eternity that can last a microsecond or a thousand lifetimes, I soar across the dark void of "the past is gone, the future is not yet here." It's called transition. I have come to believe that it is the only place that real change occurs. I have noticed that, in our culture, this transition zone is looked upon as nothing—a no-place between places. Surely the old trapeze bar was real and the new one coming towards me; I hope that's real too. But the void in between? That's just a scary, confusing, disorienting "nowhere," that must be gotten through as fast and as unconsciously as possible. What a waste! I have a sneaking suspicion that the transition zone is the only real thing, and that the bars are illusions we dream up to avoid the void where the real change, the real growth, occurs for us. Whether or not my hunch is true, it remains that the transition zones in our lives are incredibly rich places. They should be honored—even savored. Even with all the pain and fear and feelings of being out-of-control that can accompany transitions, they are still the most alive, most growth filled, most passionate, most expansive moments in our lives. And so, transformation of fear may have nothing to do with making fear go away, but rather with giving ourselves permission to "hang out" in the transition between trapeze bars. Transforming our need to grab that new bar…any bar…is allowing ourselves to dwell in the only place where change really happens. It can be terrifying. It can also be enlightening in the true sense of the word. Hurtling through the void—we just may learn how to fly.

Discussion/Goals:

Discussion focuses on how life is like a trapeze and how we experience going from one bar (one stage of life) to another bar (another stage of life). The way in which we approach challenges and change will be explored.

My Favorite Things

Materials:

Paper, pastels, crayons, markers, the song, "My Favorite Things," sung by Julie Andrews.

Procedure:

Discuss what types of things help clients feel better when they are anxious and/or depressed, e.g. a warm bath, a cup of hot cocoa, a shopping spree, reading a good book. Play the song "My Favorite Things," from the movie *The Sound of Music.* Encourage clients to sing along with the music (perhaps the words can be printed for them). Then ask clients to draw their favorite things (what helps them when they are feeling blue?).

Discussion/Goals:

Discussion focuses on self-soothing and exploring ways to cope with unpleasant situations and uncomfortable feelings.

"The Hole"[2]

Materials:

Paper, pastels, crayons, markers.

Procedure:

Read the poem "The Hole, An Autobiography in Five Short Chapters" by Portia Nelson (1993). Ask clients to share their reactions and thoughts about the poem. Creative suggestions include:

- Group members draw their interpretation of the poem.
- They draw themselves trying to get out of a hole (their depression).
- They draw the inside of one or more holes (description of the depression and specifics behind it).
- Clients draw themselves surrounded by a series of holes (problems associated with depression).

Discussion/Goals:

Discussion may focus on how clients deal with their problems and depression, and the ways in which they are trying to overcome obstacles to happiness. Repetitive patterns of behavior that are self-defeating may be examined. The end of the poem (walking around the hole) may be explored, as it demonstrates how one could have a positive outcome after many trials and tribulations. Goals include self-realization and problem solving.

The Hole

An Autobiography in Five Short Chapters

I
I walk down the street
There is a deep hole in the sidewalk.
I fall in
I am lost... I am helpless
It isn't my fault.
It takes forever to find a way out.

II
I walk down the same street
There is a deep hole in the sidewalk
I pretend I don't see it.
I fall in again.
I can't believe I am in the same place,
But it isn't my fault.
It still takes a long time to get out.

III
I walk down the same street
There is a deep hole in the sidewalk.
I see it is there.
I still fall in... It's a habit.
My eyes are open. I know where I am.
It is my fault.
I get out immediately.

IV
I walk down the same street
There is a deep hole in the sidewalk.
I walk around it.

V
I walk down another street.

Words and Pictures[3]

Materials:

Approximately 36 sheets of drawing paper, markers or colored pencils, about 40–50 index cards with various words written on them such flower, automobile, monkey, etc. The words include objects, places, people and things.

Procedure:

Mix the cards up and place them face down on the table. The first player picks a card and attempts to draw what is written on the card. He has one minute to draw. After one minute he holds up his paper and shows group members what has been drawn. Group members have to guess what it is. If someone guesses correctly, both the artist and the correct guesser get one point. If no one guesses, the artist has one more minute to finish the drawing and players have the chance to guess again. If no one guesses this time the artist doesn't receive a point and the next person has a chance. The winner is the person with the most points at the end of the game.

Discussion / Goals:

Goals include creative expression, cooperation, focusing and problem solving.

Creative Scene

Materials:

Paper, pastels, crayons, markers, pencils, pens.

Procedure:

Instruct group members to create at least two or more figures doing something. A background may be added (e.g. furniture, a house, flowers, trees, etc.). When the figures are completed ask clients to write a brief story about what is happening. Then ask the clients to share their artwork and read their story. Have them share how the artwork inspired their story.

Discussion / Goals:

Discussion focuses on the connection between the sculpture and the story, and how various symbols in both may relate to the artist. Goals include projection of feelings, being able to relate one thing to another (creative art to creative writing) and artistic expression.

Group Story

Materials:

Paper, pastels, crayons, markers, pens, pencils.

Procedure:

Group members decide on a theme for a story, and then each client adds a few lines to the story until everyone decides it is completed. The therapist or a group member writes the story on paper so that clients can refer back to it. When the narrative is finished participants are asked to draw either the part of it they liked best, their contribution to it, and/or a summary of the entire story.

Discussion/Goals:

Discussion focuses on the group members' reactions to the story, their contribution to it, and any significance the story has for them. Goals include socialization, making connections and increased self-esteem, which comes from working together as a group.

Art and Poetry[4]

Materials:

Pens, pencils, paper, pastels, crayons, markers, poetry.

Procedure:

The therapist or a group member reads a poem such as "Stopping By The Woods on a Snowy Evening" or "The Road Not Taken" by Robert Frost. Group members analyze the poem and then draw their reactions to it or a specific part of the poem.

"The Road Not Taken" is a very powerful poem. It can be used in a number of ways to help clients better understand their life path. Clients may be instructed to draw the road they took in life and the road they didn't take. Then they are asked to draw symbols representing life events on both roads (e.g. perhaps a wedding gown and children representing the road that was taken, a painter's easel representing the road not taken).

Discussion/Goals:

Poetry is rich in symbolism and provides a creative avenue to explore feelings and issues. When utilizing the poem "The Road Not Taken" clients discuss which road they chose in life and their feelings about their choice. They also discuss the road not chosen. Individuals assess their life and reflect upon accomplishments and regrets, and explore future plans.

"The Giving Tree"[5]

Materials:

Paper, pastels, crayons, markers, the book *The Giving Tree,* by Shel Silverstein (1964).

Procedure:

The group leader or a client reads this book aloud. Then group members discuss their reactions to the story and analyze various interpretations of it. The story is profound and can be interpreted in a variety of ways. In summary it is about a boy that forms a strong relationship with a tree in the forest. The tree sacrifices for the boy and over the years their relationship gradually changes. Many people relate the relationship to a parent–child bond. After discussing the book ask the clients to draw their interpretation of the story and/or the part of the story they liked best, found saddest, most profound, related to the most, etc.

Discussion/Goals:

Discussion focuses on how each individual's artwork connects to the story and relates to relationships in his/her life, especially family relationships. Questions such as, "is it a sad story, was the boy selfish, was the tree taken advantage of, did the tree sacrifice too much?" may be asked. Goals include developing empathy and self-awareness.

Famous Artists

Materials:

Books of famous artists, paper, pastels, crayons, markers.

Procedure:

Review the works of famous artists such as Georgia O'Keeffe, Vincent Van Gogh, or Picasso. Then have clients create a piece of artwork with some similarities to the artist, but using their own unique style. For instance, after they view the work of Georgia O'Keeffe have them draw the most unique flower they can think of, or have them create an abstract design that is very unusual after looking at Picasso's work.

Discussion/Goals:

Discussion focuses on everyone's unique qualities and recognition of the distinct designs that each individual creates. Goals include acquiring knowledge about major artists and appreciating one's own special style.

Before and After

Materials:
Paper, pastels, crayons, markers.

Procedure:
At the beginning of the session ask clients to draw a quick sketch representing their mood. Then guide them in a light exercise/movement experience, ending in a few deep breaths. At the end of the exercise ask them to draw their mood again.

Discussion/Goals:
Instruct clients to look for similarities and/or differences in their mood before and after the exercise. Examine how their artwork can be used as an assessment tool. Explore how movement affects mood, energy and feelings of well-being.

Expression Through Music

Materials:
Paper, pastels, crayons, markers, CD compilation.

Procedure:
During the first few minutes of an art therapy group have group members create a list of their favorite songs. Inform them that you will be making a CD from their selections and will play it for them in a future session. Make a CD from the songs. Play the CD during the next group and ask clients to draw thoughts and feelings about their favorite song or another song. Encourage them to think about rhythm, mood and lyrics.

Discussion/Goals:
Explore how music may awaken hidden thoughts and feelings. Support clients to share the effect the music had on the way they created their piece of art. Goals include creative expression and self-reflection.

Happiness[6]

Materials:
Paper, pastels, crayons, markers, the song "Don't Worry, be Happy," by Bobby McFerrin.

Procedure:

Play the song "Don't Worry, Be Happy" by Bobby McFerrin. After listening to the song ask clients to fold their paper in half and draw their worries on one side of the paper and things they are happy about on the other side of the paper.

Discussion / Goals:

Explore what makes clients feel joyful and what makes them worry. Examine methods to help control their worries. Discuss the "benefits" of worry and the difficulties many people encounter when trying to change behavior and attitudes. Cognitive distortions such as making mountains out of molehills, feeling shame, generalizing and catastrophizing, etc., may be explored.

Create a Lune

Materials:

Pencil, pens, drawing paper.

Procedure:

A lune is considered the American Haiku. It is a very simple poem and easy to teach. It consists of three lines. The first line contains three words, the second line contains five words and the third line contains three words. Either have the group as a whole develop a lune or ask each individual client to create one and then illustrate it.

Discussion/Goals:

Discussion focuses on the content of the poem and the feelings depicted in its artistic representation. Goals include creative thinking, problem solving, socialization and camaraderie (when clients work together).

This is a lune group members created and illustrated together:

> Love is here,
> Husband, wife, daughter, son, mother,
> Caring, loving, beauty.

"The Little Engine That Could"

Materials:

Paper, pastels, crayons, markers, the book *The Little Engine That Could*, by Watty Piper (1930).

Procedure:

Group members take turns reading the story "The Little Engine That Could." It is a children's story about trains/engines challenging themselves to try to go over a mountain. After the story is read ask group members to draw themselves attempting to go over a mountain (the mountain representing their obstacles to getting well and/or their depression).

Discussion/Goals:

Explore the size of the mountains drawn and where the client placed himself/herself on the mountain. Did he/she get to the top, half way up, etc.?

Discussion focuses on attitude and methods of handling life's challenges. Ask clients if they approach problems by giving up easily like some of the engines in the story, or if they persevere and say to themselves, "I think I can, I think I can," like the little engine in the story who eventually accomplished his goal.

The Recipe

Materials:

Paper, pastels, crayons, markers, pencils, pens.

Procedure:

Ask clients to write a recipe for a fulfilling life and then illustrate it.

Discussion/Goals:

Discussion focuses on the recipe and the ease or difficulty of following it. Ask clients if they follow their own recipe and/or have followed it in the past. Explore the ingredients, and whether or not the ingredients are difficult to find. For example, one young woman stated her main ingredient, a nice young man, "was not easy to come by." Goals include examining needs, desires and goals.

The Letter

Materials:

Paper, pastels, crayons, markers, pencils, pens.

Procedure:

Have clients write a brief letter or note to someone they love or admire, and ask them to illustrate the envelope. Suggest that the envelope represent the contents of the letter.

Discussion/Goals:

Discussion focuses on the way in which the artwork reflects the feelings expressed in the note. Goals include exploration of relationships, and methods to maintain healthy communication with others.

Art Therapy Bingo

I have included this game once again because it continues to be extremely popular at Princeton House. It is very common for clients to request that it be played. They find it pleasurable and relaxing, as well as challenging.

Materials:

See Procedure.

Procedure:

Take a 9"×12" sheet of drawing paper and divide it into a 3×4 grid of 12 boxes. Outline the boxes with black marker. At the bottom of each box write the name of something that is easy to draw (e.g. a tree, a sun, etc.). On the top of each box make a small circle. Make as many copies of the 9"×11" drawing paper as there are clients in the group. Next write a number (1–40) on 3"×5" index cards (one number for each card). The therapist then distributes the paper, and group members are asked to write numbers in the circles on the top of the page (any number 1–40 in any order). The therapist shuffles the index cards and calls out the numbers. Every time she calls a number the client looks to see if he has written that number in one of the circles on top of his page. If he has the number that is called he has to draw what is written (house, person, etc.) in that square to the best of his ability. The first person to fill up his boxes across or down wins (a variation of the game is the first person to fill all of his boxes wins). The winner has to show everyone all of his pictures and describe them. If the therapist desires, a small prize may be given to the winner.

Discussion/Goals:

This is a game clients usually enjoy very much. It is especially popular with the higher functioning schizophrenic patient and older clientele. It is a very non-threatening way to encourage participants to draw and learn how to sketch basic symbols. Goals include socialization and problem solving.

Broadway Star

Materials:

A CD of Broadway tunes, paper, pastels, crayons, markers.

Procedure:

Play a blend of Broadway favorites such as songs from *Gypsy, Camelot* and/or *The Music Man*. Encourage clients to sing along, perhaps making copies of the words. After a while, suggest that clients draw what it would be like to be a Broadway star. Instruct them to draw either a star that symbolizes them in some way or how they would appear on stage.

Discussion/Goals:

Clients often suffer from low self-esteem, so it is important to raise it as much as possible. This exercise encourages the client to focus on himself and allows him to be in the spotlight. Explore the type of star drawn and the significance of it. Examine the way the client depicted himself on stage (is he in the center, on the side, drawn large, small, colorful, etc.). Goals include increasing self-esteem and focusing on strengths.

"The Fable of The Two Goats"[7]

Materials:

Paper, pastels, crayons, markers.

Procedure:

Have clients read aloud the fable, discuss it, and ask them to draw themselves "butting heads" with someone else.

Discussion/Goals:

Discussion focuses on the people in the illustration who are butting heads (arguing with no results, debating, coming to a standstill). Goals include exploration of compromise, cooperation, flexibility and the ability to see the other person's point of view.

The Fable of the Two Goats

Once upon a time two proud goats stared at each other from opposite cliffs of a high mountain range. Between the cliffs lay a deep, rocky valley with a raging river at the bottom. The only bridge across the river was a fallen tree so narrow that only one goat could pass at a time. Both stubborn goats felt they had the right to cross the river first; and each immediately proceeded to walk across the slender log. The two goats met head to head in the middle of the bridge. Neither goat would give way to the other, and finally both goats fell headlong into the raging river below.

A 48-year-old newly recovering addict named Jim drew his wife and himself "butting heads." He sketched two large profiles facing each other; they both appear angry. He related the artwork and this fable to his severe marital problems. He remarked that his wife and he were having many problems in their marriage, and they were "hanging on by a thread." Jim mentioned that his wife doesn't show trust, respect, or understanding. He said he was upset because she recently stated that she loves him, but is not in love with him, and she told him she doesn't think the therapy will help him. He expressed fear that she would leave him after 28 years of marriage. Jim stated that if that happened he would be destroyed and would probably continue to take drugs/drink and most likely overdose. Group members pointed out that he has to be patient and work towards proving and improving himself, one day at a time. Jim seemed to hear and acknowledge what they said and remarked he would try to prove his worth, "but it won't be easy." He kept staring at the artwork as he shared his thoughts and feelings.

Passengers on the Bus Metaphor[8]

Materials:

Drawing paper, pastels, markers, crayons, pencils.

Procedure:

Read the following essay and then discuss with group members. Ask clients to draw their interpretation of it or any part of it, for example they may draw the passengers on the bus, the bus driver, the bus, thoughts in their mind, etc.

> Suppose there is a bus (which symbolizes your mind) and you're the driver. On this bus we've got a bunch of passengers, which represent thoughts, feelings, bodily states, and memories. Some of them are scary, and they're dressed up in black leather jackets and they have switchblade knives. What happens is that you're driving along and the passengers start threatening you, telling you what you have to do, where you have to go. "You've got to turn left," "You've got to go right," and so on. The threat they have over you is that if you don't do what they say, they're going to come up front.
>
> It's as if you've made deals with these passengers, and the deal is, "You sit in the back of the bus and scrunch down so that I can't see you very often, and I'll do what you say pretty much." Now, what if one day you get tired of that and say, "I don't like this! I'm going to throw those people off the bus!" You stop the bus, and you go back to deal with the mean-looking passengers. But you notice that the very first thing you had to do was stop. Notice now, you're not driving anymore, you're just dealing with these passengers. And they're very strong. They don't intend to leave, and you wrestle with them, but it just doesn't turn out very successfully.
>
> Eventually, you go back to placating the passengers, trying to get them to sit way in the back again where you can't see them. The problem with this deal is that you do what they ask in exchange for getting them out of your life. Pretty soon they don't even have to tell you, "Turn left"—you know as soon as you get near a left turn that the passengers are going to crawl all over you. In time you may get good enough that you can almost pretend that they're not on the bus at all. You just tell yourself that left is the only direction you want to turn. However, when they eventually do show up, it's with the added power of the deals that you've made with them in the past.
>
> Now the trick about the whole thing is that the power the passengers have over you is 100% based on this: "If you don't do what we say, we're coming up and we're making you look at us." That's it. It's true that when they come up front they look as if they could do a whole lot more. They have knives, chains and so forth. It looks as though you could be destroyed. The driver (you) has control of the bus, but you trade off the control in these secret deals with the passengers. In other words, by

trying to get control, you've actually given up the control! Now notice that even though your passengers claim they can destroy you if you don't turn left, it has never actually happened. These passengers can't make you do something against your will.

The moral of the story is: you are in charge of the bus; your behaviors and the direction you choose to live your life by. Thoughts, feelings, bodily states and memories (the passengers on the bus) will always be there and may feel threatening in many ways. However, these thoughts, feelings, bodily states and memories have never harmed you in the way you felt they would. They have only harmed you in the sense that you have made decisions that have not been true to the valued direction you want from your life. Therefore, take control of your bus.

Discussion/Goals:

Discussion focuses on the passage read, the drawings created and their meaning to the client. Procedures to stop anxiety and fear from controlling one's life may be explored. Goals include identifying self-defeating attitudes and emotions, and becoming proactive in one's life.

Loneliness

Materials:

Drawing paper, markers, crayons, pastels.

Procedure:

Tell clients to visualize this scene:

An obese teenage girl is sitting on the steps of a school building munching on an apple. The other kids are inside the lunchroom gorging on pizza, hot dogs and fries. She can hear their cheerful voices and excited cries even from the street. People pass by and she stares straight ahead munching on her apple. Couples walk by and she stares straight ahead munching on her apple. Handsome young men and pretty girls walk by and she stares straight ahead munching on her apple. One attractive young man stares at her for a few minutes. He feels sorry for her but he doesn't know what to say or do. He doesn't want to have a relationship with her but he sees she's in pain; yet he chooses to leave and go about his business. He feels it is better not to approach her because he knows a relationship is impossible. He doesn't want to hurt her; she's obviously been through enough adversity. The girl continues sitting, staring and munching on her apple.

After reading this paragraph ask clients to draw either the scene, part of the scene, the girl, the young man, or the mood of the story.

Discussion/Goals:

Discussion focuses on the clients' reaction to the story, and their feelings and associations to their artwork. The theme of loneliness is explored. Explore whether or not group members can relate to the characters in the story. Goals include exploration of loneliness, methods to combat it, and the importance of empathy.

Something Lost[9]

Materials:

Drawing paper, markers, crayons, pastels.

Procedure:

Read the following essay, discuss it, and then ask clients to draw something they have lost.

Discussion/Goals:

Discussion focuses on exploration of the artwork. Discuss what the client has lost and the impact it has made on him. Examine whether the item, feeling, person, or thing was ever returned. Goals include coping with loss and change.

What I lost

When I was first married I was very happy. I had a lovely apartment, a loving husband and many friends. I had a new job and a wonderful adventure in front of me. I knew I would be a success, as would my husband, and we would live happily ever after. My life had just begun. Every day I woke up with a smile and a sense that the world was a good place. Well, things didn't go according to the plan. As John Lennon wrote, "Life is what happens while we make other plans." Life was good the first few years but then things started to change, and not for the better. My husband started to get frustrated with his job and our financial situation; I didn't particularly like my job either. My boss was irritable and pushy; she thought she knew it all. My husband and I began arguing. It started with little things, like when he pushed his plate full of spaghetti on the floor because he wanted steak instead. Soon we began arguing constantly and it got to the point where we couldn't approach each other without yelling at one another. There was always so much tension regarding finances and our deteriorating relationship. Evan began to drink. At first I thought it was casual drinking, but then I started to see I was wrong; it interfered with his work inside and outside of the home. He never helped clean or do yard work. He left his clothes on the floor, books were strewn all over, and he seemed to mess every room he walked into. The kitchen table was piled sky high with his junk. The arguments got even worse and I was miserable. I thought I deserved better; and eventually we got a divorce. Evan didn't seem to care; in fact he seemed relieved.

All of a sudden I found myself in a tiny apartment, with very few friends. Most of our friends were originally his, and they stuck with him. I still had the same job that I disliked intensely, and a boss that was twofaced and horrible. Now I was really stuck. People my age were having babies and moving into private homes. I felt like a loser, miserable and lost. "How did this happen to me?" I lost a lot of things such as friends, a house, nice furniture, designer clothes and gold jewelry, but the most important thing I lost was my dream of living happily ever after. I grew up and realized that life is not a fairytale and I am not a princess. I lost my naivety and optimism. Now I have to work hard to change my life around and, hopefully, one day regain some of the positive feelings I used to have for a bright future.

"Stag and His Reflection"[10]

Materials:
Drawing paper, markers, pastels, crayons.

Procedure:
Read the fable and then briefly discuss it. Ask clients to fold their paper in half and on one side ask them to draw what they value in life and on the other side of the paper have them sketch what they might be critical of and/or take for granted.

Discussion/Goals:
Discussion focuses on how the moral of the story (what is most truly valuable is often underrated) relates to the artwork and the items illustrated. Examine things that clients judge or criticize that perhaps might be more appreciated (example: a messy but loving husband, a sweet daughter who is frequently late for lunch appointments, legs that work well but are full of bluish veins, etc.). Goals include exploration of values, and objects/people/things of importance.

Stag and his Reflection

A stag saw his shadow reflected in the water, and greatly admired the size of his horns, but felt angry with himself for having such weak feet. While he was thus contemplating himself, lion appeared at the pool. The stag betook himself to flight, and kept himself with ease at a safe distance from the lion until he entered a wood and became entangled with his horns. The lion quickly came up with him and caught him. Too late he reproached himself: "Woe is me! How have I deceived myself! These feet which would have saved me I despised, and I gloried in these antlers which have proved to be my destruction."

"Man and the Lion"[11]

Materials:
Drawing paper, markers, pastels, crayons.

Procedure:
Read the fable and then briefly discuss it (moral: There is always another side of the story). Ask clients to fold their paper in half and draw a person expressing one point of view on one side of the paper, and a person expressing another point of view on the other side of the paper.

Discussion/Goals:
Discussion focuses on the situations depicted and the different points of view illustrated. Examine the importance of being open and empathetic, and looking at a situation from all angles. Goals include exploration and enhancement of communication and listening skills.

Man and the Lion

A man and a lion traveled together through the forest. They soon began to boast of their respective superiority to each other in strength and prowess.

As they were disputing, they passed a statue carved in stone, which represented "a lion strangled by a man."

The traveler pointed this out and said: "See there! How strong we are, and how we prevail over even the king of beasts."

The lion replied: "This statue was made by one of you men. If we lions knew how to erect statues, you would see the man placed under the paw of the lion."

Notes

1. Used with kind permission of Carol Ross, www.abiggervoice.com

2. Copyright © 1993 Portia Nelson (1993). Reprinted with permission from Beyond Words Publishing, Hillsboro, Oregon.

3. Idea modified from the Pictionary Game by Milton Bradley.

4. Another option is just to have group members draw the road that was taken.

5. *The Giving Tree* (Silverstein, 1964) came highly recommended by Adam Buchalter. It may be purchased from www.amazon.com.

6. To find the song search ITunes software program from Apple Computer, buy the CD (which is very enjoyable), or listen to it on YouTube (www.youtube.com) a video sharing website. Variations on this project include drawing thoughts to specific songs that elicit strong responses such as "The Cat's In The Cradle" by Harry Chapin (about the relationship between a father and his son). Harry Chapin wrote many songs that are thought provoking and would be therapeutic to use in a creative group.

7. The idea of using this fable for an exercise came from Link (1977).

8. Passage from Hayes, Strosahl, and Wilson (1999).

9. The essay is fiction and written by myself in 2008 as a way to promote exploration of feelings associated with loss. I used examples that I heard from clients in various sessions to assist me in composing it.

10. www.feath.com/story/aesop.htm, accessed 03/21/09.

11. www.feath.com/story/aesop.htm, accessed 03/21/09.

CHAPTER 9

Multimedia

The use of multimedia allows clients the chance to experiment with various materials and learn how to combine an assortment of items to create a specific project or design. Individuals learn to build and put things together, to problem solve and to be resourceful. They test out supplies and try different ways of connecting objects.

A wide variety of creative projects fall under this category. Some include pipe cleaner sculpture, dioramas, marshmallow sculpture,[1] plaque design, mobiles, personality boxes, decorative items, beading design, and the obstacle course listed in this chapter. Working on these projects enables clients to learn to view things three dimensionally. Utilizing a variety of materials in three-dimensional work allows the client to view his artwork from more than one vantage point; he learns to look at it from all angles. This enhances abstract thinking. Ideally this thinking becomes generalized and helps the client better understand and view his problems, concerns and relationships in a broader, healthier and more realistic manner. It helps diminish black and white thinking. Following directions, organizing media and working on projects from start to completion enhances focusing and helps clients derive a sense of accomplishment. Individuals gain greater control and self-esteem as they learn how to problem solve and accept creative challenges.

A Modern Invention[2]

Materials:

2D open studio media (paints, pastels, pencils, markers, watercolor pencils, collage). 3D open studio materials (air-dry clay, earthenware clay, Sculpey clay, molding clay, wooden Popsicle sticks and/or a variety of wooden shapes, wood or tacky glue, found objects).

Procedure:

Ask group members to think about a problem that they and possibly others face daily. Discuss what types of inventions and technology can help to solve this problem. Suggest to clients that they may use their imaginations to develop any type of machinery, invention, etc. that may help. Explain that the invention can be anything, even if they feel it is impossible. Have group members use the materials available in the studio to create a model or prototype for their invention.

Discussion/Goals:

Discussion focuses on identifying problem areas that the group members face and to offer avenues for universality and hope. The invention serves as a catalyst for change and promotes symbolic control of problems. Goals include expression of issues, problem solving and promoting active participation in one's therapy.

Two-Dimensional and Three-Dimensional Balance

Materials:

9"×12" paper, paints, pastels, pencils, markers, watercolor pencils, collage materials, modeling clay, Sculpey clay and/or air-dry earthenware clay, wooden shapes, Popsicle sticks, found objects, stiff pieces of cardboard or foam plates/trays to work on, tacky glue.

Procedure:

Explore connections between the physical experiences of balance and the emotional experience of feeling balanced.

> **Part I:** Ask clients to consider the concept of balance and suggest they create a two-dimensional picture of what balance means to them.

> **Part II:** Next have participants create a three-dimensional sculpture of what balance means to them using cardboard, plates or trays as a base.

Discussion/Goals:

Participants discuss the similarities and differences between their two-dimensional and three-dimensional representations. They share their perceptions of what balance means literally and figuratively, and process how they can achieve more balance in their lives. Through discussion and sharing of ideas the group can then expand on their definition of balance, for example, balance is not fixed or permanent, it requires adjustment at times.

Renewal and Recovery Art

Materials:

Found objects that are considered safe for clients to use. Clean recyclable materials, bottles, boxes, tubes, bottle caps, small toys, string, glue, pipe cleaners, buttons, scraps of fabric, felt, etc.

Procedure:

Create a piece of art from used materials. Have group members define renewal. Discuss physical renewal (recycling, waiting for a new skin to form over a wound) and emotional renewal (learning coping skills, recovering from an addiction, finding new hope and meaning in life). Next, discuss the art task. Describe that creating art from objects and scraps of everyday life can be symbolic of renewal and transformation. Ask patients to create a sculpture from the objects provided.

Discussion/Goals:

Support clients to discuss their artwork and encourage them to relate it to the theme of renewal. Explore ways in which they are changing and improving their life. Goals include problem solving, self-awareness and working toward positive transformation.

Affirmation Plaques[3]

Materials:

Wooden plaque (any size depending on whether it will be a wall hanging, magnet or paperweight), sand paper, Mod Podge, acrylic paints, paint cups, paint brushes, containers of water, paper towels, scissors, magazines for collage, glue sticks, clear acrylic varnish.

Procedure:

Inform group members that they will be creating a small plaque with a positive word glued on it. Instruct clients first to sand down the plaque and then to choose paint color(s). Have them paint their plaque and allow it to dry (this takes at least ten minutes). While they are waiting for it to dry ask them to cut out letters from magazines that will form a positive word (make sure that the word will fit the piece of wood). Then instruct clients to glue the letters on the wood. Next ask them to apply a clear coat of Mod Podge on the plaque (non-toxic varnish-like substance). When the plaque is dry, magnet backs may be glued on the back of it, or if the plaque is larger, it may be used as a wall hanging or paperweight.

Discussion/Goals:

Discussion focuses on successes, as well as challenges and frustrations that arose from working on the project. Have clients share their experience organizing and completing the task, and encourage them to share the positive word selected. Goals include problem solving, focusing and increase of self-esteem.

Value Beads

Materials:

A variety of beads, string, paper, pencils and jewelry-making supplies such as clasps, crimp beads, pliers, if available.

Procedure:

Direct each group member to create a list of values that are important to them (achievement, family, leisure, inner peace, spirituality, etc.). Ask clients to choose a type of bead (color, size, shape) for each value they chose and to string them together. Jewelry or key-chains can be created if desired.

Discussion/Goals:

Discussion focuses on each group member's morals and ethics, and the reasons clients chose a specific bead for a specific value. Goals include identification of principles and beliefs, self-awareness and the practice of visual expression.

The Bank of Affirmations[4]

Materials:

One box per group member (square tissue boxes work well for this task; however, other recyclable containers, wooden boxes, or folded paper boxes will also work), scrap paper, pencils, paints, paint cups, paint brushes, containers of water, paper towels, scissors, glitter, sequins, buttons, etc. This task has worked well when divided in to two or more consecutive sessions.

Procedure:

Announce to group members that they will be creating a bank in which they will keep affirmations.

Step 1: Ask each client to write one affirmation and pass it to the therapist.

Step 2: Have each client choose a box and then paint it. He/she may also decorate it with glitter, buttons, etc. after it is painted.

Step 3: The therapist types or writes a list of the affirmations and makes enough copies for all group members.

Step 4: Clients cut out the affirmations and keep them near the box.

Step 5: The therapist then reads each affirmation aloud and group members discuss how they can use the affirmations to increase self-esteem and positive feelings.

Step 6: Clients place all the affirmations in their bank. They are encouraged to bring their bank home with them.

Discussion/Goals:

Discussion focuses on the affirmations and their value. Placing them in the bank demonstrates that positive self-talk and optimism are as "good as gold." Goals include increase of self-esteem and creation of a tangible object that encourages hope and positive feelings.

Moving On

Materials:

Cardboard boxes that can be closed (you can collect clean recyclables such as shoeboxes or foldable packing boxes prior to this task), found objects, three-dimensional collage materials, paper, paints, brushes, containers of water, clay, tape.

Procedure:

Ask group members to imagine they are getting ready to move to a new home. Suggest they create items they would like to take with them, e.g. molding a cat or prized trophy out of clay, writing or drawing wishes/hopes on paper. Each client will receive a box and will place all of their items in it.

Discussion/Goals:

Discussion focuses on the theme of moving and how clients respond to changes in their lives. The value of the items placed in the box may be examined. Goals include exploration of values, needs and how the individual prepares for "moving on" in his/her life. Towards the end of the discussion clients have the option of keeping their box open or taping it closed. The symbolism of their decision may be explored.

Silhouette

Materials:

Flashlight or projection lamp, 18"×24" paper, pencils, paints, markers, collage materials (magazines, tissue paper, foam sheets, felt, origami paper, corrugated cardboard, scrap-booking paper), glue.

Procedure:

Discuss the definition of a silhouette (a darkened image that stands out from its background). Using a flashlight set up towards a wall, or a projector, the therapist outlines the profile of each group member. Then clients are asked to fill in their silhouette with color, photos and/or collage materials. Emphasize that the silhouette will be representative of the client in some way. It might look like them and/or represent their desires, characteristics, attitudes, hobbies, etc.

Discussion/Goals:

Discussion focuses on group members' perception of how they see themselves in the world. Questions to ponder include: "Is the viewpoint of the group that 'standing out' is positive, negative, neutral, or a little of both? How do images relate to accomplishments or failures, mental illness or mental stability, etc?" Goals include exploration of self-esteem and self-awareness.

Aligning Mind and Body[5]

This idea is based on the chakra system that originated in India, more than four thousand years ago. It is believed that harmony and peace are the result of these energies being in balance. It is up to the therapist how this idea will be adapted to fit your group.

Materials:

18"×24" paper, colored pencils, rulers, clay (clay tools may be helpful but are not necessary).

Procedure:

Prior to group, the therapist will need to create or find a print of a chakra chart that is labeled with colors and descriptions. Show clients the chart and ask them to copy it (it consists of a lightly drawn figure with seven colored dots down the center). Using the chakra chart descriptions as a guideline, ask patients to create seven shapes out of clay, one for each chakra, and then place them on the drawing of the body according to how they feel at present.

Discussion/Goals:

The shapes created are used to explore how clients are feeling in the present moment, physically, emotionally and spiritually. Questions to ponder include: "What can be done to bring balance and alignment in the body and in the mind?" and "How do the shapes represent one's energy and vitality?"

Stress and Relaxation II

Materials:

Construction paper, glue, scissors, drawing paper, pastels, crayons, markers.

Procedure:

Have clients fold their paper in half, and ask them to choose two small squares of construction paper, one color that they find calming and one color that is more anxiety producing. Direct them to cut out a small shape from each color and glue the calm color on one side of the paper and the more stressful color on the other side of the page. Next ask clients to draw an illustration of what anxiety and peace represent to them next to the appropriate colors.

Discussion/Goals:

Discussion focuses on how the designs represent elements of tranquility and anxiety. Finding ways to incorporate both successfully in each individual's life so that one is not consumed with anxiety and has time for peace and tranquility may be examined. Goals include identifying factors that cause and relieve stress.

Strength II[6]

Materials:

Drawing paper, pastels, crayons, markers, scissors, glue, copyright-free images.

Procedure:

Draw or find an image of a figure, and a separate image of barbells from the Internet. Change some of the barbells by varying their size. Create one page with an assortment of barbells on it, and one page with a figure on it, and copy the pages. Distribute the pages to clients and ask them to cut out the figure and glue it on a piece of paper. Then instruct clients to choose the barbells they believe are most appropriate for the figure to hold up. Ask them to cut them out and glue them on the paper in relation to the figure. Suggest that a background may be drawn if desired.

Discussion/Goals:

Discussion focuses on the size of the barbells chosen and where they are placed on the page. Observe if the figure is holding the weights up or if they are placed on the ground near the figure. Are the barbells tiny and easy to grasp or enormous and overwhelming the figure? Ask clients to connect the picture to the way they feel about their issues and life. Goals include assessing how one is "holding up" and assessing the amount of weight clients are carrying on their shoulders (how many problems they are dealing with).

Abstract Mandala[7]

Materials:

Tissue paper, scissors, Mod Podge, markers, pencils, paper, paper plates.

Procedure:

Ask clients to outline a circle from the paper plate. Either have squares of tissue paper already cut out or ask clients to cut out the squares. The pieces may vary in size according to the desire of the client. About one and a half inch squares work well. Direct clients to glue the squares using Mod Podge or a similar type of glue onto the mandala until they fill up the circle and create a pleasing design. Then participants have the option of leaving the design as is or painting the Mod Podge over the tissue paper squares, which may make the colors blend together in a unique way, and will create a sheen. Some clients are pleased with the results; others are not, so warn them about the possible outcome.

Discussion/Goals:

Discussion focuses on the design, and the emotions and feelings it evokes in the clients. Goals include creative expression, focusing and decision making.

Pipe Cleaner Growth Collage

Materials:

Assorted pipe cleaners, scissors, glue gun, markers, cardboard or oak tag (a type of thin card), glitter, feathers, glue.

Procedure:

Instruct clients to create a collage, primarily using pipe cleaners to represent growth. The clients may interpret the directive in any way they please (they could view the suggestion as their own psychological and emotional growth or growth of objects, nature, etc.). Direct them to cut out a circular shape from the cardboard (the therapist may provide a template if so desired). The circle helps clients focus and stay within a boundary, which is helpful when focusing on this specific theme using these collage materials. In this way the collage doesn't become too spread out or too disorganized, and the degree of frustration and anxiety may be lessened. Suggest that clients may add other collage materials and markers when working on their design. Tell them that a glue gun will be used to attach the pipe cleaners to the cardboard, which will add to the stability of the design.

Pipe cleaners are used because they give the client a sense of control in that they are easily bent, curled, curved and manipulated. They allow for demonstration of growth because they can be positioned to stay straight up (using the glue gun); they can be cut into various sizes and bent in various directions.

Discussion/Goals:

Discussion focuses on the collage and the way in which it represents growth. Ask the clients if they are able to relate the collage to their growth and/or progression in therapy. Explore the way the pipe cleaners are glued onto the cardboard; examine their height, size, whether or not they are curled or curved, and the colors used. Observe whether or not there is an organization to the collage. Goals include creative expression, abstract thinking, goal planning and self-awareness.

The therapist will want to work carefully with clients when they use the glue gun. The other materials may be attached with regular glue.

This is a collage created by a 45-year-old woman named Mary who was suffering from major depression and a suicide attempt. When she began participating in the psychiatric program she felt hopeless and useless. After a divorce, the loss of her home and friends, combined with intense anxiety and depression, she moved in with her mother. Mary felt worthless and "like a loser" because at one point in her life she had a large, beautiful home, many friends and a handsome husband. According to Mary, "I lost it all." As Mary began to feel better she acknowledged that important goals were to find a job, feel useful, "reinvent her life and begin over." Mary remarked that her artwork was a reflection of this desire to "begin over." She added feathers and glitter to the collage to symbolize a more exciting life. She remarked that she placed the pipe cleaners pointing upward to represent her continued growth. Mary added some twists and curls to the pipe cleaners to represent the "turmoil and confusion" that is still present in her life. She was pleased with the results of the collage and titled it "Growing in Color."

Another client viewed his sculpture as things growing up from the earth "in many different ways." He remarked that he could relate to the artwork because he was experiencing his own personal growth: "learning, developing and budding."

Tape Design

Materials:

Thin cardboard or oak tag squares, markers, crayons, pastels, masking tape, magazine photos, scissors, glue, paint.

Procedure:

Have clients tear or cut different sizes of masking tape and place them on the cardboard in any way they please. Next ask group members to draw around the tape using crayons or markers. Then have them remove the tape and a design will be formed. Group members may now leave the design as is or fill in the empty spaces with another medium for an eye-catching effect. They may fill in the empty spaces with magazine pictures, paint or pastels.

Discussions/Goals:

Discussion focuses on the design and how the empty white space was used in the formation of it. Did the client leave the white area as is or did she continue to work with it to make a more stimulating picture? Goals include creative expression, problem solving and experimentation with materials.

"Hands That Touch The Heart"[8]

Materials:

White drawing paper, construction paper, glue, scissors, markers, crayons, pastels, red paint.

Procedure:

Instruct clients to outline their hands with any color marker they please. Have them fill in the prints with pink paint, marker, or crayon. Then tell clients to cut the handprints out. Next have them cut a large red heart from construction paper. The heart should be glued onto a large sheet of white paper with some space left around the outside. The handprints should be glued on the red heart—hence "hands that touch the heart." Finally, ask clients to write the names of two people (animals may be substituted for people) they love or have strong feelings about–one on each of the two hands.

Discussion / Goals:

Discussion focuses on relationships and people in one's life who are loving and supportive. Explore how love helps individuals deal with emotional and psychological issues.

Care Package[9]

Materials:

Small brown lunch bags, drawing paper, markers, crayons, scissors, magazines.

Procedure:

Direct clients to create a care package for themselves to use when they are not feeling well. Have them decorate the bag with positive symbols and drawings. Then direct clients to draw various things on small sheets of paper that would make them feel better when ill. Examples are DVDs, chicken soup, someone for support, a warm bed, ice-cream, Tylenol, a good book, warm slippers, cookies, being in a special room in the house, etc. They may also use magazine pictures for illustrations. After all the pictures are drawn and cut out, have clients place them in the bag to share with group members for future use.

Discussion / Goals:

Discussion focuses on examining the items placed in the bag and the ways in which they may help the individual feel better. Goals include exploring ways of comforting oneself and self-soothing.

Obstacle Course

Materials:

Drawing paper, pens, pencils, scissors, glue, markers, crayons.

Procedure:

The therapist draws or finds outlines of obstacle course objects suitable for copying. These objects may include ropes/nets, barrels, holes to jump through, logs to jump over and balance on, inclining walls, ropes to climb, a puddle of muddy water, bars to swing from, etc. The therapist makes enough copies of these objects for each group member and distributes them. The clients are asked to cut them out, glue them on the paper, and then draw a figure (any type of figure is fine) somewhere on the obstacle course engaging in an exercise. Next ask group members to complete the environment by adding more figures, trees, obstacles, etc.

Discussion/Goals:

Discussion focuses on the placement of the figure in the course (is he in the middle of it, actively attempting the tasks, is he just beginning it, etc.?). Explore the ease or difficulty the figure is experiencing. Then ask clients to relate the figure and the obstacle course to the way they are attempting to conquer their obstacles and barriers to health and recovery. Goals include exploration of ways to overcome problems and better cope with troubles and concerns.

Personal Freedom [10]

Materials:

Pre-cut bird silhouettes (birds in flight) from card paper. The birds should be about 10"×6". Open studio materials: magazines and collage materials, glue sticks, scissors, pastels, paper towels, acrylic and watercolor paints, water, brushes, paint cups, colored pencils, watercolor pencils, stampers, foam and felt, 12"x18" paper.

Procedure:

Have clients share ideas and symbols representing what "personal freedom" means to them. As the discussion progresses mention that a bird is often used as a freedom symbol, and suggest that group members use the bird outlines to create an image of personal freedom. Ask participants to trace the outline of the bird. The bird can be traced onto white or colored construction paper. Clients are directed to fill in the bird outline with magazine pictures or they may color it in themselves. Then they may create a background for the bird, with magazine photos or drawn by hand.

Discussion/Goals:

Discussion focuses on the client's personal experience while creating the freedom symbol. Encourage clients to observe the direction and flight path of the bird, and share their observations. Questions to ponder include: "What are some challenges that the birds face in their flight? How may this relate to challenges you have in gaining personal freedom?" Goals include self-awareness and exploration of independence issues.

Notes

1.   Marshmallow sculpture is described in Buchalter (2004, p. 102).

2.   Sculpey can be found in S&S Crafts (www.ssww.com) and in most art supply stores.

3.   Mod Podge, a non-toxic, varnish-like substance, can be purchased through the S&S catalog at www.ssww.com. Depending on the population you are working with and the length of the session, this project may need to be divided into two or more sessions.

4.   Depending on the length of the session it may be easier to break this project up into two or three sessions. I would suggest combining steps 1 and 2 in one session and steps 3, 4, 5, and 6 in another session. In this way the clients have more time to work on their boxes and discuss their affirmations, and the therapist has time to type and Xerox copies.

5.   www.chakra-colors.com has information and a small map of the body labeling the chakras, which you may draw and distribute to clients as a reference.

6.   Searching for "copyright-free images" on your computer will give you a number of sites where images can be downloaded and used without infringing copyright laws.

7.   At Princeton House the mandala is used in art therapy for creative expression, focusing and healing. Mod Podge is a non-toxic glue that acts like a varnish and can be purchased online at S&S Crafts (www.ssww.com). Clients may also try gluing the squares on the circle and simultaneously placing the Mod Podge on top of them for another attractive effect.

8.   Modified from a project taken from Nita Leland, Kinder Art: *www.kinderart.com*; original lesson written by Kathy Crittenden. Google: www.kinderart.com/seasons/Val11.shtml for more information.

9.   Taken from an idea suggested by Jennifer L.B. Katz, esq.

10. Another option is that the background can be created first, with images that relate to personal freedom. Then clients may trace the outline of a bird onto the background. They may add other photos or hand draw symbols to fill in the bird outline in order to complete it.

CHAPTER 10

Holiday Projects/Celebrations

These projects give clients the opportunity to acknowledge and/or commemorate various holidays and celebrations. Creatively representing them provides the opportunity to explore positive and negative thoughts and feelings that the holidays may evoke. Many clients do not have friends or family with whom to celebrate holidays such as Thanksgiving or Christmas, so they may symbolically celebrate them on paper with other group members. Negative feelings about holidays may be expressed and reviewed. In this way the client is able to express his emotions. Anxiety and loneliness are frequently lessened.

Celebrations such as birthdays are shared in various ways. Birthday murals may be created, as well as fancy individualized cards and collages representative of the individual. Clients often feel very pleased when they receive such positive attention on their special day. After one birthday mural was completed a female client remarked that it was the best birthday she ever had.

Projects may be simple like birthday or Christmas cards cut from construction paper, or as complicated as computer generated cards created by group members. What is important is the focus on the individual; he needs to feel supported and acknowledged.

Halloween Costumes

Materials:
Drawing paper, markers, pastels, crayons.

Procedure:
Suggest that clients draw the costume of their choice and explain why they chose that particular costume.

Discussion/Goals:

Examine the costume illustrated and ways in which the costume symbolizes characteristics and/or wishes of the client. Goals include exploration of identity, self-awareness and desired traits.

Birthday Collage Mural

Materials:

Magazines, scissors, glue, large sheet of mural paper, pastels, crayons, markers.

Procedure:

Group members select two to four pictures from various magazines that reflect the personality of the individual celebrating his/her birthday. They may also choose photos of gifts they would like to symbolically give him/her. A large piece of oak tag or cardboard is passed from person to person and the photos are glued on the cardboard. When all the pictures are glued in a way that is pleasing to everyone one group member writes "Happy Birthday" in a strategic place on the collage, and the mural is held up and examined by group members. Everyone gets a chance to share what he/she contributed to the mural and to wish the "special" client good wishes.

Discussion/Goals:

Discussion focuses on the reasons the photos were chosen and the way in which they relate to the "special" client. Goals include socialization, making connections, working together, and raising the self-esteem of the "special" client by acknowledging his/her special day and his/her special attributes. Group members derive a feeling of satisfaction and self-worth from giving their "presents."

Variations of the project include designing individual birthday cards composed of photos from magazines, and a birthday mural where all group members decide together where each picture goes (the pictures are glued one at a time) in order to create the design.

Clients are usually very pleased to receive one of these murals. It makes them feel connected to the group members and extremely special. A number of times clients have said that it was the best birthday celebration they ever had.

Good-bye Mural[1]

Materials:

Magazine photos, cut paper, paper, pastels, crayons, markers, scissors, glue, assorted materials.

Procedure:

Group members use magazine photos, cut paper and various other materials to create a collage that reflects their feelings about the individual who is leaving the hospital/program and the good wishes they want to give him/her.

Discussion/Goals:

Creating this project enables both the client who is leaving and the clients who are remaining in the program to say good-bye and deal with their loss. It helps the person leaving to have a personalized symbol of support from his peers. Goals include increasing self-esteem and self-worth in group members.

Halloween Masks[2]

Materials:

Pre-cut masks from art supply store or catalog, paint, markers, construction paper, glitter, sequins, buttons, feathers, pipe cleaners, glue, small wiggly plastic eyes.

Procedure:

Direct clients to create a mask that represents them in some way.

Discussion/Goals:

Discussion focuses on the way in which each person's mask is self-representative and how some individuals "hide behind their mask."

Thanksgiving Dinner Mural

Materials:

Mural paper, pastels, crayons, markers.

Procedure:

Group members take turns contributing to creating a Thanksgiving dinner. Each client chooses one thing to add to the dinner table until a complete dinner including main dish, side dishes, dessert, place settings and people at the table are drawn.

Discussion/Goals:

Many times clients do not have the opportunity to share a dinner with family and friends. In this way they symbolically have a Thanksgiving dinner with people they care about. They also have a way to vent their feelings about the holiday and take control of an unfortunate situation by creating their own dinner. Goals include socialization and making connections with others.

Christmas/Hanukkah/Kwanzaa and the Holiday Season

Materials:
Make a CD mix of a wide variety of holiday songs.

Procedure:
Play the music on low volume and ask clients to close their eyes and relax for a few minutes. Ask them to listen to the tunes and think about past holiday celebrations. Suggest they draw holiday memories and/or rituals.

Discussion/Goals:
Clients are asked to reminisce about past celebrations and the differences between "then and now." Goals include exploring holiday stressors and how to cope with difficult holiday situations, possible isolation and loneliness.

This project is particularly helpful to seniors who often experience great feelings of loss at holiday time. Reminiscing about the past can be bittersweet, but it helps them remember family and friends, and the wonderful times they had in the past. It often helps them acknowledge strengths such as putting up Christmas trees and decorating, organizing parties and cooking for large amounts of people. One depressed client stated that she used to bake six dozen cookies at Christmas time. Even though she felt unable to bake in her late seventies it made her smile with pride to remember how much work she had done in the past and how appreciated she felt.

The New Year's Resolutions[3]

Materials:
White box, magazines, scissors, glue, pencils, markers, Mod Podge.

Procedure:
Group members work together to decoupage a white box in the shape of a cigar box. They take turns gluing photos on it that are representative of goals they have for the new year. After the pictures are glued on the box, clients work together to paint a finish such as Mod Podge on top of the photos. As the box is drying clients are asked to write their new year's resolutions on slips of paper. Once the box is dry they are directed to place their resolutions in it. The box is passed around the room and each client reads one of the resolutions. The writer may acknowledge that it was he/she who wrote the resolution or he/she may remain anonymous.

Discussion/Goals:

Discussion focuses on the resolutions, hopes, goals and dreams for the upcoming year. Procedures of achieving goals may be explored.

The "February Blahs"[4]

Materials:

Paper, pastels, crayons, markers.

Procedure:

Ask clients to draw what the "February Blahs" mean to them. Discuss methods of dealing with this "malady."

Discussion/Goals:

During the long winter months many individuals become weary of the short days and cold, dreary weather. Sometimes the weather has a negative effect on these individuals. They become increasingly depressed and anxious. This project affords clients the opportunity to reflect on their feelings and try to find solutions to their depression. This project can be adapted for use during any month or time of year.

Valentine's Day: The Mended Heart Mural

Materials:

Mural paper, tan construction paper, red construction paper, glue sticks, markers, scissors.

Procedure:

Direct group members to work together to create a mural that illustrates a mended or healing heart. Suggest they utilize the media presented and encourage them to be as creative and original as they please.

Discussion/Goals:

Discussion focuses on the "mended heart" and its symbolism. Some individuals may consider Valentine's Day a time to celebrate love and relationships; however, others may focus on their feelings of loss, problems in their relationships or loneliness. Explore how the idea of a mended or healing heart applies to each person in the group and to their current relationships. Goals include expression of pleasant and uncomfortable emotions associated with the holiday, and exploration of methods to cope with conflicting and/or unpleasant feelings.

Fourth of July: Fireworks Mural

Materials:

Mural paper, markers, glue, glitter, glitter pens.

Procedure:

Have group members work together to create a fireworks display using the various materials presented. Encourage clients to recall Fourth of July celebrations from the past.

Discussion / Goals:

Discussion focuses on the reaction of group members to the completed mural and the meaning of the symbols and figures they contributed to it. Explore how they felt working as part of a team. Discuss whether memories of past Fourth of July celebrations were reflected in the way the art was created. Goals include acknowledgment of the holiday in a way that provides support and comfort, socialization, cooperation and making connections.

Group Cake Decorating[5]

Materials:

Plain sheet cake, icing new, clean, thin brushes, plastic spatula, cake decorating markers and gel.

Procedure:

Encourage group members to decide the theme for the cake illustration. Ask them if it should be realistic or abstract. Explore whether there might be certain symbols or words written on it. Then have clients take turns smoothing the icing on the cake using a spatula. Next encourage group members to take turns contributing to the overall design. When the picture is completed discuss everyone's contribution to it. When clients are ready for the group leader to cut the cake they may each have a slice.

Discussion / Goals:

This is a special project for occasions such as significant birthdays, a group member leaving a program after a long stay, or for a holiday such as Halloween. Clients often feel more positive and connected to one another after participating in this creative experience. Goals include socialization, cooperation, working together and self-expression.

Heart Collage[6]

Materials:

Construction paper (especially red and pink), scissors, glue, markers, crayons, pastels, magazines.

Procedure:

Demonstrate how to cut hearts from paper by folding the paper in half and forming half the heart. Suggest that clients cut out a variety of hearts from the construction paper and other materials to create a collage. Tell them they may also look for pictures of hearts in magazines.

Discussion/Goals:

Discussion focuses on the design of the collage and its significance for the client. Goals include sharing feelings of love, identifying significant people in one's life, and thoughts about Valentine's Day.

Notes

1. Clients enjoy this ritual so much that they usually remind this therapist at least a week in advance of the date they are leaving. They want to be acknowledged and appreciated, and share in a good-bye ceremony with their friends and peers.

2. Masks are available online from S&S Crafts (www.ssww.com).

3. The cigar-type boxes and Mod Podge (glue) may be ordered from S&S Crafts (www.ssww.com) online.

4. This project, which appeared in *A Practical Art Therapy* (Buchalter 2004), has proved to be very popular with clients so I am including it here for easy reference.

5. These items can be purchased in a variety of party supply and art supply stores such as Michaels (www.michaels.com/art/online/home) and A.C. Moore (www.acmoorder.com), and various online art stores.

6. Got to www.eHow.com and type in "make a symmetrical heart." This will take you to a page where you can then select various eHow.com sites that demonstrate how to do this.

CHAPTER 11

The Defensive Client

There are some clients who are reluctant to draw. They may feel that producing art is silly and juvenile. They may not have picked up a crayon or marker for years. "I feel like I am in kindergarten again" is a common statement made by these individuals. They frequently share stories of harsh art instructors who were critical and sometimes demeaning of their artwork. This type of client needs special understanding and patience. Insistence on drawing will only alienate the client and increase anger and anxiety. I have found that slowly introducing art is the most effective approach. Even if the client refuses to draw I will recommend that we negotiate; he is not mandated to draw but he must have a sheet of paper and markers or crayons placed in front of him. In my experience this policy works 90 percent of the time. Invariably the client picks up the crayon, begins making marks on the paper and eventually participates in the group directive. Noticing the involvement of other group members often gives him an incentive to experiment with line and color. Introducing simple creative exercises (such as abstract scribbling, doodling, using lines and outlines to create a design, and filling in pre-formed shapes) that guarantee success is an effective way to help these clients desensitize to drawing. This technique has proven successful with seniors, bipolar, schizophrenic and clinically depressed clients.

Draw Yourself as a Young Child[1]

Materials:
Drawing paper, pastels, crayons, markers.

Procedure:
During an art therapy session a client may occasionally complain that he/she feels like he is in kindergarten. If this occurs it may be helpful to ask him to share what life was like during that time period. Suggest he draws himself as a child

and include anything he remembers about that period of time (examples include toys he played with, friends, teachers, family members, games, etc.).

Discussion / Goals:

Discussion focuses on sharing what life was like at five or six years of age. Ask clients questions such as: What was fun about that period of time? How did they feel? How was their energy level? Did they worry what others thought of them? Were they curious? Discuss whether clients will give themselves permission to "let go" and enjoy themselves through artistic means. Examine what playful qualities they have maintained and the importance of allowing their "inner child" out in order to stay active and young at heart.

Photo in a Circle

Materials:

Coffee can lid, paper, pastels, crayons, markers, pencils, magazines, scissors, glue.

Procedure:

Direct clients to trace a circle using the lid of a coffee can as a template. Suggest they browse through magazines and choose one appealing photo. Have them glue the photo somewhere in the circle and then ask clients to fill in the rest of the circle with color. (You may choose to have pre-cut pictures ready to glue.)

Discussion / Goals:

Discussion focuses on sharing thoughts about the artistic process (was it difficult, challenging, frustrating, easy, fun, etc.) and then exploring reactions to the completed design. Support the client to share reasons she chose the photo and associations to the background color/s.

Stick Figures

Materials:

Paper, pastels, crayons, markers, glue, pencils, scissors.

Procedure:

Demonstrate how to draw a simple stick figure. Show how to add features and accessories such as a hat, scarf, jewelry, etc. After the demonstration ask clients to draw a stick figure that is self-representative; suggest that they use features to convey emotion. Next instruct group members to find a photo of someone who seems familiar in some way (the photo may remind them of a friend, family member, co-worker, etc.). Have them cut it out and glue it next to the stick figure.

Ask clients to create a dialogue between the two figures. The dialogue may be verbal or written.

Discussion/Goals:

Examine the size, placement, features and expression of the stick figure. Examine how the figure may reflect personality, mood and psychological state. Discuss the association between the two figures (magazine photo and stick figure), and encourage the client to share how this connection may represent a past or present relationship. Greater self-awareness will be a focus of the session.

Expressions

Materials:

An outline of a face, paper, pastels, crayons, markers.

Procedure:

Present an outline of a face on a 9"×11" sheet of paper (with just eyes and a nose drawn on it) to each group member. The therapist can draw the face or find a copyright-free image on the Internet. Suggest that clients complete the face and create a mood (joyful, sad, scared, etc.). Suggest that they can add a body and/or background to the picture if they feel comfortable doing so.

Discussion/Goals:

Having clients add to an already outlined face creates an easy and non-threatening directive. It gives them the opportunity to experiment with color and design, and to add more to the overall picture if they are feeling adventurous. Filling in the features gives clients the opportunity to express their mood and talk about feelings.

Clay Shapes[2]

Materials:

Model Magic clay.

Procedure:

Suggest that clients massage and knead the clay as a way to relieve stress. After a few minutes ask how the clay feels to the touch (is it soft/hard, pliable, cold, warm, pleasing, etc.).

Direct clients to form the clay into three balls and then have them form the balls into amorphous shapes with no special design in mind. They are supported to express themselves freely. Group members are assured that there are no judgments in art therapy and there is no "right or wrong" when working with the materials.

Discussion/Goals:

Discussion focuses on the feel of the clay, associations to the shapes, and the creative experience.

Felt Shape Design

Materials:

9"×12" or 8"×10" felt sheets, pre-cut felt shapes, either store bought or cut by the therapist beforehand. If available, sheets with a sticky back allow for easy placement.

Procedure:

Direct clients to choose a variety of shapes and place them on a felt square in any way they please. Suggest they create a design of their pleasing from the shapes and forms.

Discussion/Goals:

Clients are asked to share various elements of their design including size, shape, color and placement. Goals include experimentation, focusing and problem solving.

Scribble Design Mandalas[3]

Materials:

Paper, pastels, crayons, markers, paper plate.

Procedure:

Direct clients to outline a circle with a black marker or crayon using a paper plate as a template. Suggest they use the black marker/crayon to make a large scribble within the mandala, taking up all or most of the space. Then ask clients to fill in the scribble design with color. When the drawing is completed have the clients view the mandala from all angles and see if they can find anything that looks familiar in it (a face, animal, part of an object, etc.). Next ask clients to think of a title for the picture.

Discussion/Goals:

Discussion focuses on what clients saw in the design and how it felt to color within the circular border and/or whether they even stayed within the border. Goals include projection of feelings through images, focusing and stress reduction.

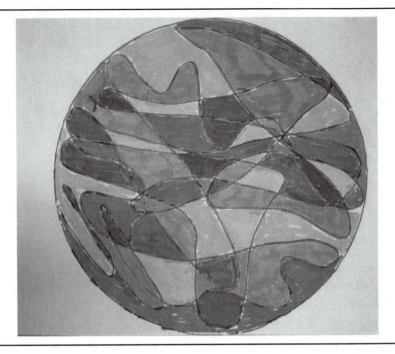

Mandala, drawn by a 68-year-old woman recovering from a deep depression. She remarked that she felt relaxed while filling in the mandala with color, and it reminds her that she has to "be bright and think positively." She titled it "Hope in a Circle."

Photo Grid

Materials:

Paper, magazine pictures, glue, scissors.

Procedure:

Prepare a grid of six squares (may be done using the computer or by hand).

Before the session cut out a variety of magazine photos that are small enough to fit into the squares of the grid. They may be photos of people with various expressions, animals, flowers, etc. Place them in a shallow box or on a plate, and allow clients to rummage through them.

Suggest that clients fill in each square with a picture that represents them in some way or that they can relate to.

Discussion/Goals:

Clients are usually more willing to be creative if there is a structure given to the page. For instance, a border drawn around the page would encourage seniors to draw more readily than on an empty page. In this way the procedure becomes less threatening. Goals include self-awareness and self-expression.

Spiral Drawing

Materials:

Paper, pastels, crayons, markers.

Procedure:

Demonstrate how to draw a spiral. Suggest that clients create a design using spirals of varying sizes and colors.

Discussion/Goals:

Discussion focuses on the connection made between the artwork and the client's emotional state. For instance, does the client feel like he/she is spiraling upward, inward or downward? Does he feel caught in a spiral, confused, going around in circles? Ask clients, "In what way is your life like a spiral?" Goals include identifying and expressing emotions and feelings.

A bipolar individual drew a series of colorful spirals varying in size and style. They were drawn in a haphazard manner all over the page; many spirals overlap. This individual stated he felt confused and his head was "like a wheel, going round and round and round." He couldn't stop thinking about certain events, and he heard music playing in his head from an opera he recently attended. When he completed the drawing the music was still in his head but he said he felt a little less stressed. On the other hand, an obsessive-compulsive woman drew a picture composed of a series of very neat and tidy spirals. They were all about the same size and color, and drawn in rows of eight. She remarked that the picture reflected her need for organization and perfection.

A depressed individual who has often been criticized by his wife and is troubled about his declining mental abilities titled his artwork, "There Are No Wrong Things in the World of Spirals."

Emotions

Materials:

Paper, pastels, crayons, markers.

Procedure:

The therapist draws a series of faces with different emotions, and makes copies for everyone. Clients are asked to fill in the face/s that represent their mood at the moment, using the color that most closely represents their mood.

Discussion/Goals:

Discussion focuses on mood and how color reflects different moods. Goals include self-awareness and expression of feeling.

Line Design I

Materials:

Paper, pastels, crayons, markers.

Procedure:

Support clients to use crayons and/or markers to practice placing all types of lines (wavy, curvy, straight) and scribbles on the paper, using a variety of colors.

Discussion/Goals:

Discussion focuses on how it felt to place the lines on the paper, and the client's thoughts about the colors used. Ask clients which are their favorite colors, their favorite part of the design, if they see anything in the design, etc. Goals include experimentation with color and line, getting used to the materials, and becoming accustomed to drawing.

Line Design II

Materials:

Drawing paper, markers, crayons.

Procedure:

Ask clients to choose five crayons or marker colors. Make one line going in any direction with each of the colors. Suggest that lines may overlap and go in various directions if preferred. Repeat this three times. Next connect them in some way. Fill in open spaces with color if desired.

Discussion/Goals:

Discussion focuses on the ease of creating a simple design and experimenting with color. Goals include creative expression, engaging in an art experience that guarantees a successful outcome and positive reinforcement.

Popsicle Stick Drawing

Materials:

Popsicle sticks, markers, crayons, drawing paper.

Procedure:

Ask clients to outline a few of the Popsicle sticks on the paper using markers. Suggest that the outlines may overlap and be spread across the page if so desired. Next ask clients to color in the outlines in any way they please.

Discussion/Goals:

Discussion focuses on the design formed and the client's use of color. Explain how abstractions are often trouble-free, pleasant and acceptable to create in art therapy groups. Goals include creative expression and experimentation.

Thinking out of the Box

Materials:

Pre-formed shapes, paper, pastels, crayons, markers.

Procedure:

Provide a variety of pre-formed shapes drawn on a sheet of paper. This can be accomplished using the computer or freehand. Suggest that clients fill in the shapes with colors that represent their feelings and/or moods. Emphasize that they need to make sure they do not stay within the lines. They should not confine themselves to a border.

Discussion/Goals:

Discussion focuses on freedom of expression and the reactions of clients to drawing in such an atypical manner. Goals include expression of mood and feelings.

Object Design

Materials:

Drawing paper, markers, oil pastels, markers, crayons, cardboard or oak tag.

Procedure:

Draw a variety of shapes on the cardboard to be used as templates (circles, squares, triangles, hexagons, etc.). Suggest that clients outline the shapes on the paper in order to create a design. They may overlap the shapes and distort them. Have them fill in the outlines with color.

Discussion/Goals:

Discussion focuses on the completed artwork. Encourage clients to observe their design from all angles and see if they can find something recognizable on it. Goals include creative expression, experimentation with line and color and abstract thinking.

Notes

1.   Occasionally a client will say that his childhood was horrible and/or he doesn't remember anything about his childhood. If this occurs suggest the client attempt to get in touch with his playful side and draw a happy/happier time in his life.

2.   Model Magic is a non-toxic clay that clients usually enjoy working with because it is easily manipulated, does not have a scent, is very clean, doesn't come off on the hands and is easily molded. The clay may be air-dried and painted. It can be purchased in an art supply store or from S&S Crafts (www.ssww.com).

3.   Mandalas: The Sanskrit word mandala means circle. At The University Medical Center at Princeton, Princeton House, the mandala is used as way to focus, heal and reduce stress. Drawing within the circle appears to be therapeutic; it quickly engages clients, it's non-threatening, and individuals usually exert a lot of energy filling in the circular shape. Nervous energy is often released, and the resulting feeling is one of peace and calm.

CHAPTER 12

Computer Assisted Art Therapy

Computer programs may be utilized to create a wide variety of creative endeavors. In addition, access to the Internet provides an endless supply of information and materials, which can be incorporated into an art project. Most simple drawing and painting programs provide similar types of functionality. You can draw specific objects easily, such as a house, tree, sun and outdoors scene. Shapes, lines, boxes, circles and more complex images may be illustrated. These objects can be filled in with colors and patterns. The images may be combined with pictures obtained from other sources (television, photos, scanner, etc.). The work can be modified by using special tools: text can be rotated, images flipped, stretched, or projected onto a surface (for example a photo of Andy Warhol can be projected onto a 3D image of a soup can). Most software palettes have a variety of tools such as paintbrushes, pencils, pens, spray cans, erasers, line makers, etc., to choose from.

Clients benefit from using the computer in a variety of ways. Many become technologically educated, which enhances self-esteem. At first some individuals are reluctant to try it, but later realize how simple and enjoyable working with the computer can be. It requires little effort to create simple images, and is non-threatening because the images can be created with a click (like Colorforms), and also deleted with a click if so desired.[1] The individual has the option and the power of saving artwork, erasing it, or even undoing individual changes. The images may be kept for future reference. Abstract designs can easily be created using simple programs, and success is nearly guaranteed. Clients gain control by deciding on the size, shape and placement of designs, and by creating projects such as their own unique person, face, or morphing exercise where one face is transformed completely. Clients problem solve and gain a sense of control by manipulating and using the various programs to create their own distinctive artwork.

Transformation II[2]

Materials:

Photoshop Elements is a powerful program from Adobe that enables the manipulation of pictures. This program has filters that allow you to totally change how a photo looks. You may change textures and styles, and distort the picture. For example, a photo of an apple may be made smaller, larger, elongated, drawn like a charcoal drawing or oil painting. A face can be widened, exaggerated; a nose could be pushed up, down and/or swirled.

Procedure:

Suggest that clients transform the photo of the person they are given to work with into an entirely different individual. Tell them that they can change all the features, some of them, distort them, add and subtract features, until they find a face that appeals to them.

Discussion/Goals:

Discuss how clients view others. What is important to them when they meet someone (their smile, eyes, teeth, overall appearance, etc.)? Encourage clients to talk about transformation and how it felt to manipulate and control this individual (photo). Suggest they share ways in which they have experienced transformation in their life or would like to be physically and/or emotionally transformed. Goals include assistance in problem solving, abstract thinking and feeling in control.

Abstract Design Reflecting Movement

Materials:

Bomomo.com (http://bomomo.com) is a website that allows free expression through the use of various widgets (a widget is a software tool that allows you to manipulate lines: for instance you can move a line in a wavy manner).

Procedure:

Encourage clients to explore the various tools and develop a design that reflects movement.

Discussion/Goals:

Discussion focuses on the type of movement presented in each design. Explore the intertwining of lines and how they create activity and energy on the page. Ask clients what feeling and mood is represented in their artwork. Suggest that clients relate the design to the movement in their lives. Explore whether they are moving ahead or stagnating. Goals include focusing, manipulating as a way to gain control, and self-awareness of one's direction in life.

Family Scene

Materials:

The Kid Pix program, from The Learning Company, is like a sophisticated electronic Colorforms set with a large collection of stamps and drawing tools such as chalk, paint, pencil and crayons. Unusual tools like spray paint, sound art, 3D shapes, and special effects like smearing are part of the program. Multiple backgrounds such as forest scenes or fantasy castles with moats are offered. Clients may use the mouse to click and place a multitude of shapes, people, flowers and other objects on a background to create a scene, design or story.

Procedure:

Create a scene of your family engaged in an activity, using the Kid Pix program.

Discussion/Goals:

Discussion focuses on family interactions and relationships. Clients are allowed to change and manipulate the scene as desired, and to save it so they are able to alter it at any time during the session or in future sessions. Allowing group members to keep changing the scene gives them greater freedom and more control. The program is easy to manipulate and an eraser is even available which makes the project less threatening. Goals include: focusing, enhancement of fine motor coordination and exploration of one's role in the family.

Group Drawing Pass With Laptop (Kid Pix Program)

Materials:

Kid Pix program.

Procedure:

Each client takes a turn adding a stamp picture to a background scene that is decided on by everyone. The laptop is passed gently from one person to another. When the group members decide the picture is completed they discuss the symbols and the completed design. As a group they title it.

Discussion/Goals:

Clients share their contribution to the overall picture and discuss what the images represent to them. Goals include socialization, making connections, cooperation and increased communication with others.

Advertisement

Materials:

Picasa is a free photo manipulation program from the makers of the Google search engine. It allows you to change colors, tints and textures (can make a picture appear grainy), and transforms designs to black and white if desired. Text and borders may be added.

Procedure:

Tell clients that they will be creating an advertisement for a product (e.g. healthy and very tasty vegetables) and/or message (e.g. smoking is dangerous) that can help people in some way. Make a grouping of photos for clients to choose from. Have them choose photos, with a click of the mouse, that will represent their product. Encourage them to think of a name for the product and write it somewhere in the advertisement. Suggest they select one or more additional pictures and text that will go along with the theme. They may create a border as part of the advertisement.

Discussion/Goals:

Clients share their advertisement and its features. Have them explore how it would benefit themselves and others. Goals include problem solving, abstract thinking and gaining control/taking charge (through manipulation of program tools and being the designer of a new product).

Announcement

Materials:

Microsoft PowerPoint is a part of the Microsoft Office suite of programs (you can use any version). Although meant for creating presentations, this program can be used for the creation of a variety of artwork. Many different template styles are available that will provide an assortment of backgrounds. Titles and subtitles can be added, and pictures may be taken from the clip art section. Pictures may be found under a variety of areas in clip art including groupings of "emotions pictures" or "entertainment pictures." Words can be designed in a decorative manner.

Procedure:

Direct clients to create an announcement using the Microsoft tools about an achievement or something else that they are proud of (people in their life, objects, jobs, special qualities such as thoughtfulness and helpfulness, volunteer positions, etc.).

Discussion/Goals:

Discussion focuses on the achievement and how it was presented. Clients may be encouraged to discuss how they feel using the various tools to create their design. Goals include problem solving and increased self-esteem.

Mood Design

Materials:

Microsoft Paint is the free painting accessory that comes with almost every version of Microsoft Windows.

Procedure:

Instruct clients how to select and use appropriate tools to create abstract designs representing mood and feeling. They may use spray paint, pencil, brush, etc.

Discussion/Goals:

Discussion focuses on the mood and feeling depicted in the design, and the colors and shapes chosen. Goals include focusing and expression of emotion.

Abstract Design using Microsoft Paint and Mixed Media

Materials:

Microsoft Paint, paper, pastels, crayons, markers.

Procedure:

Ask clients to create a design on half of the page using the Microsoft Paint program. Have them print it and then continue it using markers and/or pastels, crayons, etc.

Discussion/Goals:

Discussion focuses on the use of the tools and media, and the finished product. Explore how it felt to combine the media. Goals include experimentation, expression of feeling and problem solving.

Computer Assisted Collage

Materials:

Copyright-free images, Microsoft Paint program.

Procedure:

1. Choose a desired image from the Internet.

2. Select it (click the image using the right side of the mouse).

3.   Copy the image.

4.   Go into Microsoft Paint with the image.

5.   Keep repeating this procedure until the client has selected all of his/her photos.

6.   Now the pictures may be manipulated, placed in various locations (e.g. near each other, on top of each other, overlapping, etc.) until the collage is completed.

7.   Then click "Save" and "Print" if desired.

Discussion/Goals:

Discussion focuses on the procedure and the meaning of the collage. Goals include problem solving, being able to follow a series of directions, creative thinking and expression of issues, emotions and feelings.

Many variations of this collage can be presented. Themes can be similar to magazine and mixed media collages: people, emotions, happiness, family, hobbies, etc.

Changing the News

Materials:

Microsoft Paint program.

Procedure:

Suggest to clients that they can create a news article of their choosing or change an existing article to represent their feelings and/or point of view.

1.   Open up the Microsoft Paint program.

2.   Go to a news site such as CNN.com (www.cnn.com) and make the window large enough to contain as much of the chosen news article as possible.

3.   Hold down "Alt" key and press "Print Screen" key on the keyboard.

4.   Go back to the Paint program, go to the "Edit" menu and select "Paste."

Now anything on the screen can be modified. For example, you can go back to Google Image, search for an image, right click the mouse, and press "Copy Image." Then go back to the Microsoft Paint program and paste. Text can be deleted, crossed out, erased, modified, etc. Clients can put in their own headlines, statements, comments and photos.

Discussion/Goals:

Clients are provided an avenue to vent issues and concerns. They gain a sense of control by "being in control of the news." Discussion focuses on the manner in which they change the news and the modifications and ideas presented.

Complete the Picture

Materials:

Copyright-free images pencils, pens, paper, pastels, crayons, markers.

Procedure:

Select and print out a photo that is thought provoking. You may do this before the session or with the clients. For instance, if you work with seniors, a photo of a group of seniors laughing together would lend for discussion and exploration. After a photo is chosen make copies for everyone. Ask clients to either write what they think is happening in the photo and/or complete it by adding an environment around it.

Discussion/Goals:

Discussion focuses on how the picture is completed and what clients believe is being conveyed in the photo (projection of feelings is common). Goals include problem solving, creative expression and introspection.

Design a Person

Materials:

Website: Moonjee.com (www.moonjee.com)

Procedure:

Clients are introduced to this simple, free program and shown how they may choose the size and shape of the face they want to create. They may select whether the person will be male or female, thin or fat, young or old, attractive or strange looking. The size, color and shape of the eyes, ears, nose and mouth are designed by the client, and may be changed at any time. The ethnicity and hair can be created, as well as moles and piercings. Group members have the ability to decide what type of person they created and what his/her personality will be like. They may even make their person look like a movie star such as Tom Cruise.

Discussion/Goals:

Discussion focuses on the feeling of power one has while deciding what type of features and style the individual created will possess. Explore how the creation reflects the client. Continue the discussion by asking group members questions regarding their "person." Explore lifestyle, friends, family, age, marital status, job status, etc. Have group members relate their own lifestyle, etc. to that of their "person." Goals include experiencing a sense of control, projection of feelings, creative expression.

Notes

1.   Colorforms are toys produced by the Colorforms Corp. They are paper thin, die-cut vinyl sheets, images and shapes that can be applied to a cardboard background. The images stick to the cardboard by static cling, and can be repsitioned to create new scenes and designs.

2.   An even more powerful program with more features is Adobe Photoshop, but it is much more expensive, at about $500.00. Photoshop Elements can be purchased online or in computer oriented stores for about $50.00.

CHAPTER 13

Murals

Mural making is beneficial for clients because it promotes togetherness, unity, cooperation and socialization. It provides a forum for discussion, decision making and problem solving. It is often less threatening for clients because everyone participates and everyone is considered equal in their contribution to the artwork. Creative thinking is enhanced as group members decide on the theme for the mural and the way it should be approached. Clients are given the opportunity to observe and reflect on their own work as well as the work of others. Their comments are welcomed because of the non-threatening nature of the directive and because clients understand that everyone is an integral part of the artistic process.

Groups may be led in a variety of ways. Murals may be placed on the wall, floor or table depending on the flexibility of the clients and layout of the art room. The clients or therapist can decide whether group members will draw at the same time or participants will take turns, one person drawing at a time. A theme may be given, group members may decide on the theme, or a mural may be drawn in a spontaneous manner. Any number of materials may be utilized: paint, markers, pastels, finger paint, clay, magazine photos and collage materials, etc. depending on the capabilities, desires and needs of the clientele. When the mural is hung up after the session is over, clients often enjoy observing it, pointing out their contribution and analyzing it with peers. Their self-esteem and a sense of belonging greatly increase.

Mural of Faces

Materials:
Large sheet of mural paper, markers, crayons, pastels.

Procedure:
Place the paper on the table so that all group members can draw on it at the same time, or place the paper on the wall and have clients stand and sketch. Direct

clients to draw a face expressing an emotion, on their share of the paper. When the faces are completed have them add an abstract symbol/shape next to their face that reflects the emotion conveyed.

Discussion/Goals:

Discussion focuses on reactions to the mural as a whole and to each individual's contribution. Explore the emotions portrayed and how the clients relate to them. Discuss the importance of facial expressions when communicating with others. Goals include exploration of communication styles and identification of mood and feeling.

Footprint Mural[1]

Materials:

Large sheet of mural paper, paper, pastels, crayons, markers, pencils, pens.

Procedure:

Place a large sheet of paper on the floor. Inform clients that they will be participating in designing a group footprint mural. Ask group members to decide where they would like to place their foot to be outlined for the mural. Have clients outline each other's foot if they are comfortable to do so (they will keep their shoes on). Next ask participants to write their name on their footprint. Suggest they fill in the print in any manner they please. Depending on the size of the room and the clients' ability to bend down, the prints may be filled in on the floor or the paper may be brought up on a table.

Discussion/Goals:

Discussion focuses on the placement of the footprint (in the middle of the paper, to the side, at the end, etc.), the way it is drawn (bold, bright, filled completely in, lightly sketched, detailed, scribbled, etc.) and how the client felt working on this project. The footprint will be seen as a representation of the individual. Goals include exploration of self-esteem, placement in the group, socialization, cooperation and communication.

Mandala Self-Esteem Mural[2]

Materials:

Paper, pastels, crayons, markers, paper plate, large sheet of oak tag.

Procedure:

On an 11"×14" sheet of paper ask group members to outline a circle using a paper plate as a template. Have them draw a small rectangle in the middle of the circle. In the rectangle ask clients to write one or more positive characteristics about themselves. Suggest that they decorate the surrounding circle to represent various aspects of their personalities (e.g. red swirls for happiness, blue skies for peace and harmony, etc.). When the circles are complete instruct clients to cut them out and glue them on a large sheet of oak tag. As a group decide where each circle should be placed.

Discussion / Goals:

Discussion focuses on the positive traits of each individual and exploration of each unique mandala. Group members are encouraged to observe the mural in a variety of ways; first as a single unit and then as a composition of many distinctive mandalas. The mural may be used to explore how group members see themselves as well as how others view them. Procedures to acknowledge, maintain and increase self-esteem should be explored.

"A Patch of Life" Mural

Materials:

Mural paper, markers, squares of 3"×3" or 4"x4" construction paper, glue, scissors.

Procedure:

Everyone chooses a color and then receives a square of 3"×3" or 4"×4" construction paper, which will be pre-cut by the therapist. Clients will be asked to draw one patch of their life (one part of it) on the paper. When the pictures are completed clients decide together as a group where to place them on the paper, and then they are glued together to create a paper quilt.

Discussion / Goals:

Discussion focuses on the quilt and each individual's representational square. Goals include socialization, sharing, group cohesion and increased self-esteem by being part of a team.

Decades Mural

Materials:

Large sheet of mural paper, markers, crayons, pastels.

Procedure:

Have clients decide which decade they wish to focus on. This will depend on the ages of the group members, for example, seniors will most likely choose the 40s or 50s, and baby boomers may select the 60s or 70s. Suggest that participants draw items, clothes, symbols, words and things they would find during that period of time. For example, if the 60s were chosen symbols might include bell bottom pants, a guitar, flower (flower power, a hippie, the Beatles, etc.).

Discussion / Goals:

Discussion focuses on the era, the symbols drawn and reminiscing about that period of time. Goals include socialization, cooperation and unity. Reminiscing brings individuals together and enhances self-awareness, and often brings about positive feelings.

Collage—Mural Figures

Materials:

Sheet of white or brown paper large enough to spread over a long table, paper, glue sticks, crayons, markers.

Procedure:

The therapist outlines the figure of a person on paper (approximately 8"×10"). Group members receive this figure, cut it out and fill it in to represent themselves in some way. They are asked, "Fill in the figure to represent some aspect of yourself." Group members are then instructed to paste the figure onto the paper wherever they like. They are asked to create an environment around the figure and connect the figure to at least one other figure using this environment (e.g. a row of flowers or trees may be drawn from their figure to the next figure).

Discussion / Goals:

Connections with others are focused upon. Discussion may include the following questions:

1. What do you think of this mural? (Feelings that may arise upon observation.)

2. How do you feel about your figure placement (e.g. is it in the center, way to the side, etc.)?

3. How do you feel about the connections others made to your figure?

4. Which figures did you connect to and why?

5. How many figures did you connect to?

6. How did you feel about making the connections? Was it easy, difficult, etc.?

7. How does the artistic connection represent the type and amount of connections you make in your life?

8. Is it easy or difficult for you to form relationships with others?

9. What are some of the ways to form relationships?

10. What are the obstacles that stand in your way of forming bonds with others?

11. With whom would you like to improve your relationship?

Connections Mural

Materials:

Large sheet of mural paper, scissors, glue, small one- or two-inch squares of colorful paper already cut or have clients cut the squares.

Procedure:

Instruct clients to create an abstract or realistic design using the squares. As the design progresses suggest that they think of a way to connect it to that of the individuals sitting near them.

Discussion/Goals:

Discussion focuses on the illustration and the way in which the client made connections to his/her peer/s. Goals include abstract thinking and formation of relationships with others.

The Dinner

Materials:

Mural paper, markers, crayons, oil pastels, one small and one large paper plate.

Procedure:

Instruct clients to place the large paper plate in front of them and the small plate next to it. Have group members outline the plates onto the mural paper. Direct them to draw their favorite dinner on the large plate, and their favorite dessert on the smaller plate. Ask clients what type of centerpiece they would like in the middle of the table and have participants work on one together or elect one individual to design it. Everyone helps to create the tablecloth by deciding what type of pattern should be drawn, for instance, clients may decide on a polka dot pattern, and everyone draws the polka dots where they are sitting until the background of the paper is filled in and the tablecloth is completed.

Discussion/Goals:

Discussion focuses on the dinners and desserts drawn, and the clients' thoughts and associations to the food. Memories of past holidays and dinner parties are often evoked. Group members discuss how it feels to be enjoying their "meal" together. Goals include socialization, connectedness and cooperation with peers.

Favorite Place

Materials:

Mural paper, markers, crayons, oil pastels.

Procedure:

Direct clients to draw their favorite place. Suggest that it could be located in the home, a vacation site, a store, theatre, etc. When the drawings are completed, ask group members to view the mural and place a check mark near one place, other than their own, that they would like to visit or experience.

Discussion/Goals:

Discussion focuses on everyone's favorite place and the sites where clients placed their checks. Ask group members the reasons for their choices. Goals include exploration of leisure activities, broadening one's horizons about future possibilities and experiences, and sharing and making connections with peers. The sharing of experiences raises self-esteem and increases positive feelings.

Welcome Mural

Materials:

Mural paper, markers, crayons, oil pastels, glue, scissors, magazines.

Procedure:

Ask group members to work together to draw and/or cut out figures, symbols, pictures and words that are welcoming for newcomers to the group. Examples include: smiling faces, suns, flowers, trees, people holding hands, the word "welcome" written in a decorative manner, etc.

Discussion/Goals:

Discussion focuses on the drawings and pictures, and the way in which they represent a warm welcome for new clients. Group members are supported to share their contributions to the mural and their thoughts about working together. Goals include socialization, cooperation, problem solving and connecting with others.

Unity

Materials:

Mural paper, markers, crayons, oil pastels.

Procedure:

Instruct clients to place their hands on a sheet of paper and outline them. Next ask group members to fill the outlines in with color and design. Have them cut the hand outlines out and place them on the mural paper so that everyone's hands are touching. Ask participants to work together to title the mural.

Discussion/Goals:

Discussion focuses on reactions to the completed mural and the similarities and differences of the hand designs. Celebrating each individual's uniqueness might be explored. Goals include socialization, cooperation, unity and cohesiveness among group members.

Confronting Issues

Materials:

Mural paper, markers, crayons, and oil pastels.

Procedure:

Discuss the term, "Hiding your head in the sand." This expression, transferred to human behavior in the early 1600s, alludes to the belief that ostriches burrow in sand thinking they will not be seen because they cannot see. In fact, however, when they do this, they are consuming sand and gravel to aid their digestive system. Explain that it means retreating and not allowing oneself to face problems and/or responsibilities, pretending not to acknowledge the responsibilities, pretending not to see the dilemma.

Next provide outlines of heads with blank faces or have clients draw their own. Instruct participants to fill in the face so that it is self-representative in some way. Ask clients to cut the heads out when completed and to place a piece of masking tape on the back of the heads (make it into a circle, doubled over, positioned so that the tape will not be seen from the front). Next have participants work together to draw a layer of sand spreading across the length of the paper. Finally ask them to take their faces and place them somewhere in relation to the sand (over the sand, in the sand, under it, etc.).

Discussion / Goals:

Discussion focuses on the type of face drawn, its expression, and the placement of it. Discuss how the placement may represent one's willingness or unwillingness to face problems and challenges and move ahead. Goals include self-awareness and exploration of attitudes toward getting well.

Famous Artists Mural[3]

Materials:

Crayons, markers, oil pastels, colored pencils, a large sheet of brown wrapping paper, tape, art books that focus on well-known groups of artists such as the Impressionists.

Procedure:

Xerox copies of the drawings of artists such as Monet and Manet: These copies should be outlines, line drawings that are not filled in. The clients are given the copies and the art books, and are asked to fill in the outlines of the Xeroxed scenes and shapes with color. They can use the art books for inspiration or guidance. Then they are asked to cut up their pictures so that they are left with the main image of the page, e.g. the person, house, garden. Next participants are asked to glue this image onto a large sheet of mural paper. The last step is for group members to draw a background for their illustrations.

Discussion / Goals:

Goals include socialization, increased communication with peers, focusing and problem solving. Discussion may center on working together, and exploring how the placement of one's artwork on the large sheet of mural paper relates to one's feelings about oneself in the home and group environment.

Notes

1.   This project is suitable for a group where the members have known each other for a while, can bend down, and feel comfortable working together. To enhance the experience clients may create an environment around their footprint.

2.   Mandala is Sanskrit for circle. In my art therapy groups mandalas are used primarily for focusing, stress reduction and healing.

3.   This project is a variation of one presented to patients at the University Medical Center at Princeton by Jill Gardner, ATR-BC. It was included in *A Practical Art Therapy* (Buchalter 2004).

CHAPTER 14

Miscellaneous

The following projects include an assortment of ideas. They often combine materials and aim to enhance creative expression, problem solving and abstract thinking. Some of the directives might fit into the Combining Modalities chapter but I chose to place them here because of their uniqueness and specific usage in therapy groups. Projects such as mood shapes, puzzle designs, identity paperweights and magazine mosaics are included.

The projects introduce clients to various ways of expressing issues, thoughts and emotions. Clients learn and expand on their cognitive skills as they decide how to approach the directives and relate to them after they are completed.

Moods

Materials:

Drawing paper, markers, crayons.

Procedure:

The group leader distributes a page filled with assorted outlined shapes of varying sizes. This could be hand drawn, Xeroxed, or drawn on a computer and printed off. Some of the shapes should have sharp edges and some should be circular with smooth edges. Clients are asked to choose one or more shapes that symbolize their present mood. Then they are asked to fill in the chosen shapes with colors that also represent their mood.

Discussion/Goals:

Discussion focuses on each client's mood and issues that relate to his/her frame of mind. The association between mood and the shapes and colors chosen is an important part of the discussion. The leader may help clients examine mood changes and stability of mood.

Flower Arrangement[1]

Materials:

Paper, glue, scissors, markers, pastels, crayons.

Procedure:

Each group member chooses one color and draws a flower filling up an 8"×10" or 9"×12" sheet of paper. The flowers are cut out and glued to a vase that one person is selected to draw (or that has been drawn by the therapist).

Discussion/Goals:

Discussion centers on the meaning of the colors chosen and the result of the group effort. Goals include socialization, cooperation and making connections.

Reactions to Photos

Materials:

Photos of different people, or computer clip art copied on paper, markers, colored pencils, drawing paper.

Procedure:

Glue or have clients glue photos onto drawing paper (you may use clip art instead and Xerox the pages). Draw a rectangle underneath the pictures. The photo and the rectangle should each take up about half the sheet of paper. In the rectangle ask clients to draw their reactions to the photo using color and design.

Discussion/Goals:

Discussion includes reactions to the photo, memories and/or associations it may bring about. This exercise is a helpful way to bring about increased conversation in a quieter group. Feelings about various aspects of life are explored depending on the content of the photo. This is beneficial to seniors who enjoy relating to photos and reminiscing. For example, one photo was of an elderly man and woman sitting with their heads touching on a couch. Associations in a group of seniors included marriage, death and divorce. People spoke about their 40- and 50-year marriages, their children and their families.

Weariness

Materials:

Colored construction paper, drawing paper, scissors, glue, markers, crayons, pastels.

Procedure:

Instruct clients to select an appropriate color, and then cut or tear a shape that represents weariness (tiredness, fatigue, apathy, disillusionment). Direct clients to glue the shape on the paper in any way they please. Next ask group members to draw a figure near the shape and have them title the picture.

Discussion/Goals:

Discussion focuses on the connection between the shape and the figure, and how they represent weariness. Examine the size, color and positioning of both forms. Explore what type of situations cause fatigue and examine ways to increase energy and zest for life.

This project is particularly helpful for individuals who have low energy and are doing little at home except sleeping and watching television. It gives them the opportunity to express their feelings while illustrating their fatigue. In this way they can observe and study their weariness, and look for coping mechanisms. Individuals are given the ability to regain some control and direction in their lives.

A client named Emma cut out a small gray shape and placed a tiny stick figure under it. She remarked, "The shape is lifeless and dull." The figure (herself) "is being sucked under the gray shape." She stated that the figure has no energy or motivation to move it, but "if I don't do something it will overpower me and destroy me." As the session progressed Emma acknowledged the need to regain her emotional and physical strength by taking one step at a time. She remarked that it will be difficult to change, but she will try her best, and she will begin by calling a friend. Emma made a pledge with group members and myself to do this. The artwork allowed Emma to take a step back and analyze her situation; the illustration of her predicament was right in front of her. She couldn't deny the seriousness of her situation, and so she began to do something about it. She took her first step.

Figures in an Environment

Materials:

Small foam barrel shapes. These pieces are called "Foamies" 3D shapes; they look like mini marshmallows and can be purchased at www.darice.com (item no. 1035–80). Other materials include one sheet of 9"×12" paper or larger if so desired, markers, crayons, pastels, glue, scissors, wool, felt, tiny wiggly eyes found in craft stores, and any other collage type materials that are available.

Procedure:

Suggest that clients create a self-representative figure from the Foamie shape. Clarify that it need not look like them, but it should be symbolic of their personality in some way (for example: is it smiling or sad, colorful, fancy or ordinary, etc.). They can use the materials to create a face, hair and even feet. When the figure is completed direct clients to glue it on a white sheet of paper and draw an environment around the figure.

Discussion / Goals:

Explore the design of the figure and ways in which the figure is self-representative. Discuss where it is placed on the paper (for example: is it in the center, or bottom, side or corner of the paper) and what meaning the placement has for the client. Examine the significance of the environment drawn and relate it to the client's relationship to his/her environment. Goals include self-awareness and increased insight into one's present situation.

Shared Affirmation Cards[2]

Materials:

Sturdy index cards, acrylic or watercolor paints, paint cups, brushes, water, paper towels, pencils, pens (if you feel it would be beneficial for your group, you can print a list of affirmation examples, see below).

Procedure:

Affirmations help clients change negative self-talk into something more positive. Creating a tangible piece of art that reflects the feeling of the chosen affirmation can enhance its effectiveness and increase self-esteem.

Discuss what affirmations are and explore how they can be used to help people think more optimistically and develop self-worth. Ask clients to offer examples of positive statements that reflect their strengths and values. Inform clients they will be designing affirmation cards that can be kept in their purse, pocket or wallet as a reminder to stay positive. Ask each client to create two affirmation cards, one that they will keep for themselves and one that they will make specifically for the group. Suggest that the affirmation be written on one side of the card, and an abstract design that reflects the affirmation be created on the other side of the card. When completed, each group member shares both cards. One card will be kept by the group member and the other card will be placed in the center of room. The group cards in the center of the room may then be distributed so that each group member receives another affirmation to keep.

Discussion/Goals:

Discussion focuses on the affirmations and exploration of how they can increase self-esteem, help change one's outlook, and decrease anxiety. This project provides clients tangible support; the positive statements can be repeated or written out in times of stress. The cards may serve as transitional objects that connect clients to the group and give them a sense of comfort and belonging.

Affirmations

I will enjoy life
I will value myself
I will think positively
I will do my best
I am worthy of love
I am a valuable person
I won't give up
I will believe in myself
I will move forward
I will take one step at a time
I will be mindful
I will think positively
I will transform negative thoughts into positive ones
I decide my self-worth
I have inner strength
I will focus on my achievements
I will count my blessings each day
I will make new friends
I will help others
I will focus on what is in my control and not dwell on what is out of my control
I will look towards the future and not dwell on the past
I will accept life's challenges
I will not give up
I will treat myself as well as I treat others
I will do what I have to do
I will pat myself on the back for a job well done
I will regard today as a present.

Balloon Stress Ball

Materials:

5" balloons, buckets of sand, small funnels that fit into the opening of the balloons, paper or plastic cups that hold at least 4 ounces of sand (or 24 teaspoons), teaspoons, scrap paper.

Procedure:

Explain that group members will spend the first half of the session creating a balloon stress ball and then they will utilize the ball for the second half of the session.

> **Part I:** Allow each patient to choose a balloon. Have them obtain a teaspoon, a cup and scrap paper. Then direct each person to scoop 24 teaspoons of sand into their cup. Using the funnel(s), direct clients to pour the cup of sand into the opening of the balloon. Tie knots at the end of each balloon.

> **Part II:** Suggest that clients hold the balloon in their palm and close their palm and fingers around it first lightly and then at increasing pressures. Emphasize that each client should squeeze only to a degree that is comfortable to him or her. Have group members switch hands or use both hands and allow for a few minutes of silence when the exercise is completed.

Discussion/Goals:

Clients are empowered while creating their own stress reducer that may be taken home (as long as the therapist deems it safe for the specific client to have it). Discussion focuses on the experience of creating the balloon stress ball and describing how it felt while squeezing and manipulating it.

Identity Paperweight[3]

Materials:

Wood block, paint, wooden letters, Mod Podge, glitter, sequins.

Procedure:

Present group members with a small square block of wood. Provide wooden letters with the first initial of each client's first name. These letters are inexpensive and may be purchased in most art supply stores such as Michaels or A.C. Moore. Direct clients to paint the letter, put it aside, and then paint the block of wood. When the wood block is dry suggest that clients use glitter, permanent makers and/or stickers to decorate it in such a way that the design represents the client. Finally have the patient glue his/her initial on the wood. When everything is dry Mod Podge may be painted on to provide a clear finish. If glitter is being used, ask clients to put it on after the Mod Podge is applied.

Discussion/Goals:

Clients usually feel a sense of accomplishment after completing this project. The way they view themselves is often reflected in the manner in which they worked, and the design of the paperweight. The therapist may suggest that group members observe the colors, symbols drawn and the degree of work put into the project. Clients with higher self-esteem often create a bolder, more detailed piece of art while clients with lower self-esteem put less effort into the work, which is usually painted quickly without thought to color or design. Discussion focuses on the manner in which the project was completed and the client's reaction to it. Goals include problem solving, focusing and self-reflection.

The Band-Aid Box

Materials:

Paper, pastels, crayons, markers, pencils, pens, Band-Aid boxes, scissors.

Procedure:

Collect as many Band-Aid boxes as there are clients. Give each group member an empty box. Have them write or draw problems and/or hurts on small sheets of paper (about the size of Band-Aids) and have them put the papers in the box. Allow each client to have a chance to share a few of his hurts and explore methods of "bandaging them up." The therapist may want to give each client a Band-Aid to show support and symbolize healing after he shares his issues.

Discussion/Goals:

Discussion focuses on exploration of problems and emotional wounds, and methods to heal them. Goals include learning about nurturing and self-care.

Family Members as Animals[4]

Materials:

Drawing paper, magazines, glue, scissors, markers, crayons, pastels.

Procedure:

Instruct clients that they will be creating a family scene, but they will substitute animals for family members. Ask them to cut out photos of animals that may represent family members in some way, e.g. if a client's husband yells a lot she may choose a lion to represent him. Next have group members create an environment around the animals.

Discussion/Goals:

Encourage clients to share the way in which the family members are similar to the animals chosen. Discuss how the animals interact, where they are placed on the paper, and what they are doing. Encourage exploration of family relationships and dynamics.

Relationships II

Materials:

Drawing paper, markers, crayons, pastels.

Procedure:

On a sheet of 8"×10" paper outline the figure of a man and a woman with black marker (or search for the outlines on Google Image). Have clients cut out the figures, decorate them (add features, hair, clothes, etc.) and glue them on a piece of drawing paper. Instruct group members to create an environment for them.

Discussion/Goals:

Discussion focuses on the placement of the figures, their environment, how they are designed, and exploration of their relationship. Questions such as, "Who are these individuals, what is their connection, are they content, can you relate to them, etc.?" may be asked. Goals include exploration of relationships and connections with others.

Magazine Mosaic[5]

Materials:

Magazines, scissors, glue, water, small dish, old paintbrush, construction paper.

Procedure:

Instruct clients to find a large picture in a magazine and cut it out. Tell them to either tear apart or cut the picture into separate pieces. After they are finished cutting up the pictures tell them to dilute some glue with water in a small dish. Have them apply the diluted glue to the back of the torn pieces, and glue the pieces of the picture back together on a piece of construction paper. Instruct group members to leave some space between the pieces. This makes the picture look like a mosaic.

Discussion/Goals:

Discussion focuses on the mosaic and the artists' reaction and associations to it. Discuss how the image selected remains essentially the same even though it is presented in a different manner. Generalize this concept to the theme of transformation. Discuss how the essence of a person remains the same even though he/she may look or feel different due to age, weight gain or loss, illness, hair loss, or physical and psychological illness. Goals include self-awareness and retaining one's core and strengths.

Rorschach Pictures

Materials:

Paper, pastels, crayons, black markers.

Procedure:

Discuss what Rorschach pictures are; you may find examples on the Internet. Use search engines such as Google to find pertinent information. Ask clients to make up three Rorschach-like designs each. Emphasize that everyone will observe different images in the designs. When they are completed have them take turns guessing the possible meanings of each other's prints.

Discussion/Goals:

Discussion focuses on the various interpretations of the prints and the artist's interpretation of the prints. Goals include problem solving, abstract thinking, creativity and socialization.

Puzzle Pieces[6]

Materials:

Cardboard or oak tag, markers, crayons, scissors.

Procedure:

On large sheets of oak tag (11"×14" or so) have clients create the outline of a jigsaw puzzle. The leader might show clients a typical puzzle so they get an idea how to create their own puzzle. If need be, the leader might provide an already outlined puzzle. Clients are instructed to color in all of the puzzle pieces and then cut out the puzzle pieces. They may be asked to create a picture that has meaning to them and/or to express an emotion, or tell a personal story using the puzzle pieces. The puzzles are switched and group members put together each other's puzzle.

Discussion/Goals:

Discussion focuses on the reaction people had to putting together the puzzle (was it difficult, challenging, easy, etc?). Organizational skills and eye–hand coordination can be assessed using this procedure. Clients explore the meaning of the puzzles and how each puzzle reflects each member's thoughts, issues and concerns. Goals include problem solving, focusing and enhancement of abstract thinking.

Notes

1. Construction paper or tissue paper, as well as watercolor or acrylic paint may also be used to create the flowers and vase.

2. This project may need to be divided into two or more sessions depending on the population you are working with and the length of the session

3. Mod Podge is a clear, non-toxic varnish-like substance, which can be purchased from S&S Crafts (www.ssww.com) or art supply stores such as Michaels and A.C. Moore (store locations online at www.michaels.com/art/online/home and www.acmoore.com).

4. This project is especially useful for clients who are reluctant to discuss feelings. They are usually less threatened and n more willing to speak about the animals. It is easier to be critical about a baboon than about a brother, sister or parent.

5. Modified from an exercise presented from www.howstuffworks.com (type in magazine mosaic).

6. Variations include using one large piece of oak tag and creating a group puzzle. In this case the puzzle would provide enough pieces so that each group member would draw something meaningful on their own puzzle piece. Group members would work together to complete the puzzle. Socialization, focusing and problem solving would be emphasized.

CHAPTER 15

Open Art Studio

Artists have long learned, generated inspiration, and created in an open studio, an artists' workroom where ideas can thrive and transform amongst a group. As a therapeutic approach, authors have written that the open art studio provides an active environment of creation in which art is kept central, rather than acting mainly as a tool for verbal therapy (Allen 1992, 1995, 2008; Cahn 2000; McGraw 1995; McNiff 1995; Moon 2002; Wix 1995, 1996). The space that evolves in an open art studio offers the participants personal refuge and a place to venture towards individual goals. At the same time, it is a collaborative community where art is accessible to diverse populations and accommodating to those of differing functioning levels.

There are many open art studio approaches, although most methods agree that participants are able to choose the materials and the creative direction that shape their art (Allen 2001; Block, Harris and Laing 2005; Deco 1998; Moon 2002; Vick and Sexton-Radek 2008). Trial and error are encouraged and modeled by the facilitator who often creates side by side with the group. The facilitator provides support or assistance when requested, or as it appears to be needed by remaining in tune with the group process. Towards the end of the session, the facilitator can approach participants individually, or a group discussion can evolve. In my practice using the open art studio approach with adults diagnosed with a mental illness and often co-occurring addiction, I have found these three factors to be integral: (1) a safe, creative environment, (2) the ability of the group leader to facilitate the use of art materials and techniques in a flexible and often non-traditional manner, and (3) training and experience working with the population involved in the open art studio.[1]

My undertaking is to meet each participant where their art can unfold, whether through fine arts, crafts, modern media, or a blending of the arts. Some participants come into the open art studio and begin with complete independence. However, more often I have found that individuals come in with an intention for creative expression but state that they do not have a clue where to begin. These participants can be offered starting points from which they can then formulate their own expressions. For this chapter, I have compiled a list of **starting points** that you can make available in the open art studio in addition to your standard art materials. At the end of each starting point I've offered **example applications**.

Clay Experimentation[2]

Materials:
> At least two different types of clay. You may also need paper towels and a container of water depending on the clay used.

Procedure:
> Encourage participant to try squeezing, kneading and rolling each type of clay in their hands. Ask them to consider the differences in hardness, moisture, texture and temperature. If interested, the participant can try to create a simple object (such as an apple) out of each type of clay to help them decide which type they prefer.

Example Application:
> A participant may state that he wants to create in clay, but fears making a "mess." If given the opportunity to become more familiar with the unique qualities of different types of clay, he may be more comfortable with initiating his own expression.

Effects with Water[3]

Materials:
> At least one of the following: water-soluble oil pastels, watercolor pencils, or watercolor paints. Paper, brushes, a container of water and a spray bottle.

Procedure:
> Encourage participant to draw shapes or designs on the paper and to color them in using the water-soluble media. Then ask them to use a brush to add varying amounts of water to the areas they have colored. They can also experiment with spraying water over their art.

Example Application:
> A participant may state that he feels comfortable with drawing, but would like to expand on his creative expression. Watercolor paints and water-soluble media offer a wide range of intensity and subtlety in color. These media can also add

spontaneity to one's art process due to the unpredictable manner in which the water affects the art.

Jewelry Design[4]

Materials:

Beads, monofilament (fishing line), clasps, scissors, needle-nose pliers.

Procedure:

Encourage participants to experiment with different colors and patterns prior to stringing the beads. If participants desire, offer a demonstration for how to complete a bracelet or necklace by adding a clasp.

Example Application:

Often participants suffering from depression will show a lack of interest in personal appearance, and we observe that interest in self-care slowly returns as their mood lifts. I have found that one method of supporting participants in this transition is to offer a way for them to create wearable art. In addition, this currently popular craft often piques the creativity in participants who have an interest in color theory, design, or functional art.

Wooden Birdhouses[5]

Materials:

Pre-assembled wooden birdhouses, sand paper, acrylic paints, brushes, glue. Decorative ideas such as: rub-on transfers, stencils, design stickers and 2D/3D collage items can be useful, but are not necessary.

Procedure:

Offer interested participants their choice of birdhouse. If requested, you can offer some education about sanding, painting and/or design. Encourage participants to complete the birdhouse in any manner that they wish using the materials available in the open art studio.

Example Application:

Often participants enter the studio with the goal of obtaining a leisure skill or practicing stress reduction. Wooden crafts offer a structure and steps that can be done at home, while also offering opportunities for individual expression and design.

Emotional States

Materials:
   Choice.

Procedure:
   Create a visual representation of an emotion using any of the materials in the studio.

Example Application:
   Visual expression of feelings is often the main task of a structured art therapy session, and in the open art studio it can also be important, if not inevitable! However, the main distinction is that in the open art studio it is the participant who chooses this form of art.

Found Object Art/Assemblage

Materials:
   A collection of clean recyclables in a variety of sizes and interesting remnants (small plastic toys, ticket stubs, packaging materials, old audio-tapes), balsa wood, fabrics, nuts and bolts, glue, wire, string/yarn.

Procedure:
   Encourage the interested participant to look through the objects/materials and assemble a number of them in any way that he chooses. The participant can also include other media in the studio such as paint.

Example Application:
   A participant may state that he is having trouble focusing his mind on the present. The participant may be able to practice remaining in the here-and-now of the open art studio with art that is physically active and mentally stimulating. Found object art and assemblage art may also engage a participant in gaining more flexible thinking and perspective taking.

Wooden crafts. A 45-year-old female, with bi-polar disorder and alcohol dependence, put together this model of a tank and designed it in pastel paint colors with rub-on transfers. The transfers included the words, "pursue," "seize the day," "live," "truth," "laugh" and "imagine." Participant described her art as a symbol of something feminine with physical and emotional strength.

Projector Drawing[6]

Materials:

A 2D image or line drawing of the participant's choice, a projector, a wall or screen that paper can be affixed to, paper, pencil.

Procedure:

Assist the participant in setting up the projector as necessary by following your projector's instructions. This may involve hanging the paper on a wall or screen, and adjusting the size and placement of the projected image. Have the participant outline the projected image or draw the portions of the image that are desired.

Example Application:

A participant may bring in a picture or symbol that is meaningful to him and state that he has tried many times to draw it without avail. This technique has been used in art education and graphic design and can assist the participant in recreating the meaningful image. Also, enlarging/reducing an image or images may be just the foundation for a piece of art that may combine or change these images. (Please be aware of copyright laws pertaining to the duplication of images.)

Pastel Color Field[7]

Materials:

Pastels, paper; paper towels or one's fingers can be used for blending.

Procedure:

Encourage the interested participant to use the pastels to fill the entire paper with large areas of solid color without adding any detail. Encourage the participant to experiment with the range of intensity and subtlety that can be attained with each pastel color.

Example Application:

One participant I worked with, a 56-year-old man diagnosed with bipolar disorder, who was also legally blind due to macular degeneration (a medical condition which results in a loss of vision in the center of the visual field due to damage to the retina), came to the open art studio wondering how he could participate in visual expression. He reported that he could see large areas of color, but that the sharp edges of things were not clear to him. This participant expressed great benefit from using pastels to create color fields and this allowed him to share the way in which he experienced the world with others.

Crochet[8]

Materials:

Worsted weight yarn and a size H crochet hook are good for beginners, scissors, and a yarn needle.

Procedure:

Offer interested participants a demonstration of the slip knot, starting chain and single or double crochet. Encourage participants to practice rows without the necessity of completing a project. If they feel ready to begin a simple project, a scarf can be suggested.

Example Application:

I have had participants state the desire to learn a type of needlework because of its tie to their family traditions. At other times, participants request needlework because it can be functional, or because they feel that it can be used as a leisure skill and method of relaxation. I find that crochet has been an ideal starting point for these participants because you can begin using just a few materials, and the steps can be demonstrated clearly.

Starting With Pre-Drawn Outlines and Designs[9]

Materials:

Pre-printed outlines and designs, colored pencils, markers (pastels, watercolor pencils and paints can also be offered).

Procedure:

Allow the participant to choose an outline or pre-drawn design that he has an interest in completing. Have the participant fill in the outline in any way that he chooses.

Example Application:

This starting point can help a participant who is new to art and the open art studio to overcome the initial anxiety of being in a foreign environment. Often if they are able to begin with a pre-drawn structure, participants can experience the relaxation and grounding that art activity can bring forth with less self-judgment. As they do this, they may also become aware of other types of art available and they may observe how other participants express themselves. The utilization of pre-drawn outlines in the open art studio is one method of experimenting with color and image awareness that may help participants gain the confidence to formulate their own expression.

Signs and Plaques[10]

Materials:

A piece of wood, cardboard or paper (any surface on which you can create a sign or a plaque). The participant's choice of additional materials available in the open art studio.

Procedure:

Encourage the participant to put a written expression onto the sign/plaque in some manner. It can be in any format (e.g. a phrase, a quote, poetry, or by stringing words together randomly).

Example Application:

Some participants state discomfort with visual art expression, but feel strength in their written expression. It may help for them to begin by bridging the written and visual in this manner. Participants can also be encouraged to illustrate or create a visual image to go with the written material on the plaque.

Create a Zine[11]

A zine is a hand-made booklet combining the idea of a newsletter, personal journals, collage, drawing, doodling, etc.

Sign. A 48-year-old male with bi-polar disorder, post traumatic stress disorder (PTSD), and poly-substance abuse created this sign by starting with a phrase and adding imagery to illustrate and emphasize the meaning. Participant stated that his art was a reminder that he had the capability to stop his negative thinking.

Materials:

A pen/pencil, photocopy paper. Other media can be incorporated as the participant chooses.

Procedure:

Encourage the participant to begin by journaling, doodling or creating a magazine collage. It may be helpful to suggest that the participant create a border around a blank piece of paper and then fill in the space with writing, drawing or collage.

Example Application:

This activity would be suitable for a participant who comes in feeling heightened emotions or having strong opinions on a subject and has the desire to vent in a quick, free-flowing and often unedited expression. Teenagers and participants who enjoy comic/cartoon drawing or graffiti art have gravitated to this starting point. It is important for the facilitator to be aware of the participant's ability to contain him or herself and be safe, and for the participant to have an understanding of how the material may impact others who read it.

Color Mixing[12]

Materials:

Acrylic paints in a variety of colors, a palette, wooden craft sticks, water containers, brushes, paper.

Procedure:

Have the participant experiment with mixing colors freely. Encourage him to choose at least two colors and to mix them together with a craft stick. If requested, demonstrate simple color mixing. The participant can be encouraged to remember or write down the formula he used to make colors that he may want to use in the future. If the participant desires, he can create a painting or design using the colors he has mixed.

Example Application:

A participant may enter the studio with the desire to use certain colors connected to a thought, feeling or memory. He may want to use these specific colors in his art. Another application may be for a participant who has an interest using colors, highlights and shadows in his art, but has not had a chance to experiment with color mixing and shading for its own sake.

Community Bulletin Board[13]

Materials:

A cork board or other type of bulletin board hung on the wall of the open art studio. Art materials are chosen by the participant.

Procedure:

Encourage the participant to create a piece of 2D art, a sign, or a flyer that he feels would be appropriate for the community bulletin board. If he wishes, he can post his creation.

Example Application:

Having a community bulletin board can be a way to unify the community that develops in the open art studio over time. Participants who feel certain types of art making have been valuable can share their ideas, feelings and inspirations on the bulletin board. In addition, those who are new to the open art studio will have the community board as a resource and a starting point of their own art.

Notes

1. These three factors are of key importance in the open art studio because, as the facilitator, you are responsible for offering safe and appropriate media choices specific to the population, and you will need to anticipate the potential for adverse responses or regression by individuals during the art-making process.

2. I have found it ideal to have the following types of clay available in the studio: (1) air-drying clay such as Creative Paperclay or Model Magic by Crayola, (2) polymer clay such as Sculpey or Fimo, (3) non-drying modeling clay such as Plasticine, and (4) pottery clay such as NASCO earthenware.

3. Brands that offer water-soluble supplies include Portfolio Series and Loew-Cornell. For more information on watercolor techniques, see Metzger (1996).

4. Additional supplies that I have found useful in my work with adults include: an assortment of glass and ceramic beads, beading wire, crimping tubes and crimping pliers. These materials can be purchased at reasonable prices through the NASCO catalog, or at art stores such as Pearl Paint, Michaels, and A.C. Moore.

    Websites such as Fire Mountain Gems (www.firemountaingems.com) and Beadage (www.beadage.net) can offer the facilitator more information on creating jewelry.

5. The use of wooden birdhouses in the open art studio at Princeton House Behavioral Health partial hospitalization program in Princeton, NJ was first implemented by art therapist, Jill Gardner.

    Pre-assembled birdhouses come in a variety of sizes and styles. I have found that they regularly go on sale at arts and crafts stores such as Michaels and A.C. Moore. In addition, variations of this starting point can utilize wooden boxes, shelves, plaques, frames, model kits, etc.

6. Variations of this starting point may include the use of grid drawings and charcoal or carbon transfers.

    Prism, Tracer and DesignMaster are art projectors that can be purchased through the Artograph at www.artgraph.com website.

7. Mark Rothko and Clyfford Still were prominent color field artists if you would like to learn more refer to the book, *Colour as Field* (Belz and Wilkin 2007), or do an online search using the artists names.

8. Variations of this activity may include other types of needlework such as knitting, embroidery, cross stitch, latch-hook, etc. Plastic lacing (also known as lanyard and gimp) is another technique that does not require a needlework tool.

Instructional videos such as *Crochet Made Easy*, an interactive CD-ROM (available from Coats and Clark at www.coatsandclark.com/Products/Publications/Learn+How) can help you get started. Also, various websites such as that of Lion Brand Yarn (see http://Learntocrochet.lionbrand.com) may have additional information that will assist you.

9. Variations of this starting point could be to offer velvet posters, stained glass art or plastic sun catchers.

    Pre-printed outlines or designs can be drawn by the therapist, printed off the internet, or obtained from design books. Dover Publications has an excellent range of coloring books for participants of all ages and backgrounds (see http://storedpublications.com/by-subject-coloring-books.html).

10. A variation of this starting point can be done using photography. Photographs taken by participants or brought in by participants can be affixed to painted plaques with glue and clear varnish. This can be applied as a starting point for individuals who come in with an interest in photography, and a desire to connect this interest with different types of visual art expression. Please be aware of the Health Insurance Portability and Accountability Act (HIPAA) and confidentiality regulations if using any type of photography in the open art studio.

11. It is possible for individuals to photocopy and share their zines if appropriate. To learn more about creating zines, see Block and Carlip (1998).

12. If you are not sure what colors to offer, the simplest would be to offer the primary colors (red, blue and yellow), black and white. Any type of paint can be substituted for this starting point.

    Many materials can be used as a palette; it does not have to be store bought. Options include plates (plastic, Styrofoam, ceramic), waxed paper or palette paper, or scraps of your cardboard recycling.

    Simple color mixing would include: mixing of primary colors to get secondary colors, mixing secondary colors to get tertiary colors, adding white to create tints, and adding black to create shades.

13. Other methods of celebrating and acknowledging the community that develops in the open art studio could be to have an open studio community exhibit or art slideshow. Please be aware of the Health Insurance Portability and Accountability Act (HIPAA) and confidentiality regulations that may apply when photographing or displaying an individual's artwork.

References

Allen, P.B. (1992) 'Artist-in residence: An alternative to "clinification" for art therapists.' *Art Therapy: Journal of the American Art Therapy Association 9*, 1, 22–29.

Allen, P.B. (1995) 'Coyote comes in from the cold: The evolution of the open studio concept.' *Art Therapy: Journal of the American Art Therapy Association 12*, 3, 161–166.

Allen, P.B. (2001) 'Art making as spiritual path: The open studio process as a way to practice art therapy.' In J.A. Rubin (ed) *Approaches to Art Therapy: Theory and Technique* (Second edition). Philadelphia, PA: Brunner-Routledge.

Allen, P.B. (2008) 'Commentary on community-based art studios: Underlying principles.' *Art Therapy: Journal of the American Art Therapy Association 25*, 1, 11–12.

Block, D., Harris, T. and Laing, S. (2005) 'Open studio process as a model of social action: A program for at-risk youth.' *Art Therapy: Journal of the American Art Therapy Association 22*, 1, 32–38.

Belz, C. and Wilkin, K. (2007) *Color as Field: American Paining, 1950–1975 (American Federation of Art)*. New Haven, CT: Yale University Press.

Block, F.L. and Carlip, H. (1998) *Zine Scene: The do it yourself guide to zines*. US: Girl Press.

Buchalter, Susan (2004) *A Practical Art Therapy*. London: Jessica Kingsley Publishers.

Cahn, E. (2000) 'Proposal for a studio-based art therapy education.' *Art Therapy: Journal of the American Art Therapy Association 17*, 3, 177–182.

Deco, S. (1998) 'Return to the open studio group.' In S. Skaife and V. Huet (eds) *Art Psychotherapy Groups*. London: Routledge.

Frost, R. (1916) "The Road Not Taken" *The Mountain Interval*. New York, NY: Henry Holt and Co.

Frost, R. (1923) *Stopping by the Woods on a Snowy Evening*. New York, NY: Henry Holt and Co.

Hayes, Steven D., Strosahl, Kirk D. and Wilson, Kelly G. (1999) *Acceptance and Commitment Therapy*. New York: Guilford Press.

Link, A.L. (1997) *Group Work With Elders*. Sarasota, FL: Professional Resource Press.

McGraw, M.K. (1995) 'The art studio: A studio-based art therapy program.' *Art Therapy: Journal of the American Art Therapy Association 12*, 3, 167–174.

McNiff, S. (1995) 'Keeping the studio.' *Art Therapy: Journal of the American Art Therapy Association 12*, 3, 179–183.

Metzger, P. (1996) *The North Light Artist's Guide to Materials and Techniques*. Cincinnati, OH: North Light Books.

Moon, C.H. (2002) *Studio Art Therapy: Cultivating the Artist Identity in the Art Therapist*. London: Jessica Kingsley Publishers.

Nelson, Portia (1993) *There's a Hole in my Sidewalk*. Hillsboro, OR: Beyond Words Publishing.

Piper, W. (1930) *The Little Engine That Could.* New York, NY: Platt and Monk Publishers.

Silverstein, S. (1964) *The Giving Tree.* New York, NY: HarperCollins Publishers.

Vick, R. and Sexton-Radek, K. (2008) 'Community-based art studios in Europe and the United States: A comparative study.' *Art Therapy: Journal of the American Art Therapy Association 25,* 1, 4–10.

Winnicott, D.W. (1988) *Human Nature.* New York: Schocken Books.

Wix, L. (1995) 'The intern studio: A pilot study.' *Art Therapy: Journal of the American Art Therapy Association 12,* 3, 175–178.

Wix, L. (1996) 'The art in art therapy education: Where is it?' *Art Therapy: Journal of the American Art Therapy Association 13,* 3, 174–180.

List of Projects